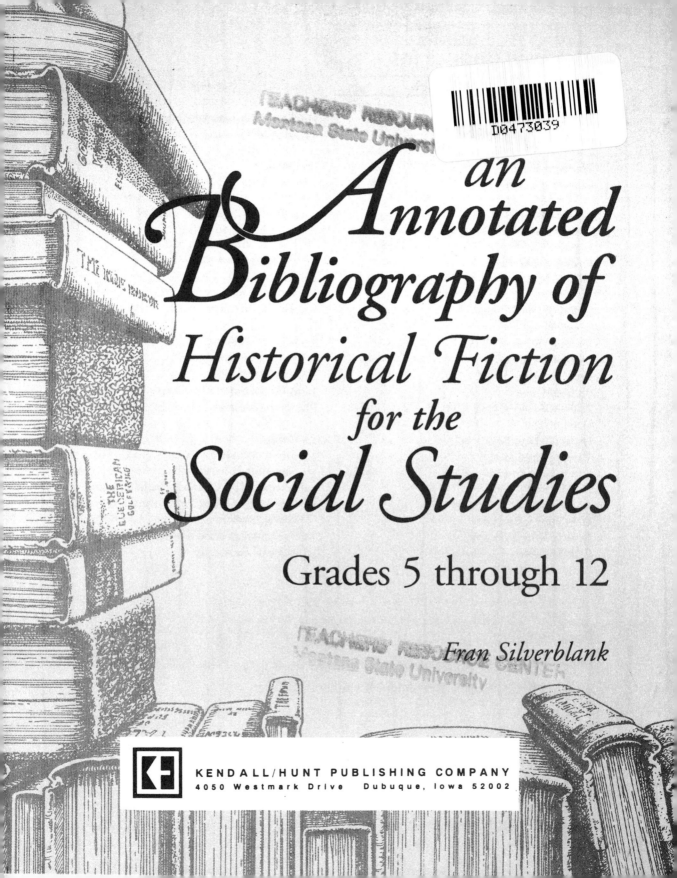

an
*Annotated*
*Bibliography of*
*Historical Fiction*
*for the*
*Social Studies*

Grades 5 through 12

*Fran Silverblank*

**KENDALL/HUNT PUBLISHING COMPANY**
4050 Westmark Drive    Dubuque, Iowa 52002

# National Council for the Social Studies

Editorial staff on this publication: Salvatore J. Natoli, Pamela D. Hollar, M. Angela Olson
Design: Dan Kaufman

Library of Congress Catalog Card Number: 92-71246

Copyright © 1992 by NATIONAL COUNCIL FOR THE SOCIAL STUDIES
3501 Newark Street, NW • Washington, DC 20016-3167

ISBN 0-8403-7516-6

Printed in the United States of America
10  9  8  7  6  5  4  3

# Contents

## United States History

In this section the following symbols indicate:
■ African American Experience
● Native American Experience

## World History

In this section the major location of the story is indicated in brackets following the title.

## Appendix

# About the Bibliography

## Purpose

This two-part annotated bibliography is for teachers who want to use historical fiction to supplement their curriculum. It is often difficult to identify such books because unlike "biography," which can easily be found under "B" or "920," they are simply part of the general fiction collection.

There is little doubt that historical fiction teaches history effectively because readers can identify with convincing people. Readers can enter a different place or time and see events and ways of life different from their own. The writers of historical fiction may choose to write about great people and important events or ordinary people who live in a particular period and find their lives affected by the times.

Nevertheless, writers of historical fiction adhere accurately to the facts of history but embellish the unadorned facts with a thousand tiny details that bring feeling, passion, and perception to their scholarship. In other words, in the context of a story, they present the issues, customs, values, economics, and landscapes of a period with truth, conviction, and clarity.

In the books chosen the aforementioned are givens. The annotations, therefore, simply indicate the content of the story.

## Availability of Books

Books were checked in two ways: (1) if they were available through the Suffolk County Library System in Suffolk County, New York (61 member libraries) and (2) if they were listed in *Books in Print 1990*.

For each entry, publishers and the most recent date of publication are given.

## Arrangement of Annotations

Most classes have students with a wide range of interests and abilities. The books, therefore, are arranged by time periods and suggested reading levels are indicated. A few books span two or more time periods and in such cases the annotations appear in the time period in which the story primarily takes place.

## About the Author

Dr. Fran Silverblank is Professor of Education, Dowling College, Oakdale, New York. Prior to assuming her present position, she taught for many years at New York University. She has published widely in educational journals such as *Phi Delta Kappan*, *Educational Leadership*, *California Educational Research*, *Clearinghouse*, *Urban Education*, *Reading Improvement*, and *College Student Journal*, mainly on teaching reading, language arts, and literature. She has teaching experience at every level, from kindergarten through graduate school.

# An Annotated Bibliography of Historical Fiction for the Social Studies: Grades 5 through 12

Fran Silverblank

## Introduction

This bibliography is for teachers who want to use historical fiction to supplement the social studies curriculum. It is often difficult to identify such books because, unlike biographies, they are simply part of the general fiction collection.

Historical fiction—whether focusing on famous people and important events or on average people—teaches history effectively because readers can identify with convincing people, enter a different place or time, and see events and ways of life different from their own. Writers of historical fiction adhere to the circumstances of history but garb the unadorned facts with tiny details that bring feeling, passion, and perception to their scholarship. In other words, they present truthfully, clearly, and convincingly in the context of a story, the issues, customs, values, economics, and landscapes of another time.

A large body of literature supports this point of view. I recommend the following readings that would be most helpful if read in the order presented.

Kulleseid, Eleanor. *Literature, Literacy, and Learning.* Chicago: American Library Association, 1989. For teachers interested in a literature-based curriculum, this is a good beginning. The authors present a theoretical framework and discuss the characteristic elements of such an approach. Includes suggestions for further reading.

Norton, Donna. *Through the Eyes of a Child.* Columbus, Ohio: Merrill Publishing Co., 1987. See chapter 10, "Historical Fiction."

Egoff, Sheila. *The Republic of Childhood.* Toronto: Oxford University Press, 1967. See part 3, "Historical Fiction."

Glazer, Joan I., and Gurney Williams III. *Introduction to Children's Literature.* New York: McGraw-Hill, 1979. See chapter 8, "Historical Fiction: Literature's Light on the Past."

Aiken, Joan. "Interpreting the Past." *Children's Literature in Education* 16 (Summer 1985): 67–83.

Meltzer, Milton. "The Social Responsibility of the Writer." *New Advocate* 2 (Spring 1990): 155–158.

Little, Jean. "The Writer's Social Responsibility." *New Advocate* 3 (Spring 1990): 79–88.

Laskey, Katherine. "The Fiction of History: Or What Did Miss Kitty Really Do?" *New Advocate* 3 (Summer 1990): 157–166.

For teachers looking for ideas on how to incorporate literature into the social studies curriculum, I recommend the following books.

Cline, Ruth, and William McBride. *A Guide to Literature for Young Adults.* Glenview, Ill.: Scott, Foresman, and Co., 1983. See chapter 7, "Literature in the Curriculum."

Cullinan, Beatrice. *Literature and the Child.* New York: Harcourt Brace Jovanovich, 1981. See "Teaching Ideas" in chapter 9, "Historical Fiction and Biography."

Norton, Donna. *Through the Eyes of a Child.*

Columbus, Ohio: Merrill Publishing Co., 1987. See "Involving Children in Historical Fiction" in chapter 10, "Historical Fiction."

Reed, Arthea. *Reaching Adolescents: The Young Adult Book and the School*. New York: Holt, Rinehart and Winston, 1985. See chapter 9, "The Social Studies Curriculum and the Young Adult Novel," which includes the use of thematic units, individualized reading, and social problems novels. It also offers sample units, a bibliography, and a discussion of books.

Rudman, Marcia Kabakow. *Children's Literature: An Issues Approach*. New York: Longman Publishing Group, 1984. See "Try This" sections in chapter 5, "Heritage," and Chapter 9, "War."

Stewig, John Warren. *Children and Literature*. Chicago: Rand McNally and Co., 1980. See "Sharing Historic Fiction with Children" in chapter 8, "Trips through Time: Historic Fiction."

Tiedt, Iris M. *Exploring Books with Children*. Atlanta: Houghton Mifflin Co., 1979. See chapter 9, "Literature for the Social Studies," which addresses using trade books, the contemporary problems approach, and the area study approach. It also contains activities that incorporate the use of books.

# Criteria for Selecting Books

## Theme

- The theme (or themes) are fundamental to the human experience enabling the reader to link the past and the present.
- The theme is understandable to the age group for which the book is written.
- The people, places, and issues of the time period come alive for the reader.

## Plot

- The story relates to action and conflict resolution illustrative of the time period.
- The plot development holds together the events, characters, settings, and conflicts.
- The chronological sequence of events clearly communicates the passage of time.
- The historical facts are effectively woven into the story.
- The pace of the story reflects the rate of living at that time in history.
- The author uses details to highlight time, place, social order, and human interest elements.

## Characterization

- Characters come alive in the context of history.
- Characters are portrayed with accurate, faithful human details that intensify their distinctness against the background of the period.
- The characters convey the book's overall themes.
- Today's readers can identify with characters from the past because of their generality and convincing portrayal.
- The characters' speech, dress, mind-set, conduct, and manners accurately mirror the time period.
- Words, phrases, dialogue, idioms, and expressions are appropriate to the time and the author uses them adeptly.
- The story does not contradict historical records.

## Setting

- The author uses historical details to enhance the reader's sense of life in the past.
- The historical details are vivid enough to fashion a clear background so that the story can move along in a satisfying way.
- Major and minor details of people, time, places, costumes, creeds, and views accurately reflect the time period.

## Availability of Books

Books included in this bibliography were listed either in *Books in Print 1990* or were available through the Suffolk County Library System in Suffolk County, New York. This system has sixty-one member libraries and an excellent, extensive children's collection. Before purchasing books, Suffolk County librarians generally consult sources such as the following:

- *The Alan Review* (Assembly on Literature for Adolescents, National Council of Teachers of English; published three times per year)
- *Booklist* (American Library Association; twenty-two issues per year)
- *Books for the Teen Age* (New York Public Library; annual)
- *Bulletin for the Center of Children's Books* (University of Chicago Graduate Library School; monthly except August)
- *Junior High School Library Catalogue* (H. W. Wilson Co.; cumulated every five years with annual supplements)
- *Senior High School Catalogue* (H. W. Wilson Co.; cumulated every five years with annual supplements)

In addition, virtually all librarians turn to the *School Library Journal* (R. R. Bowker) which employs a panel of approximately four hundred librarians who review books appropriate to their backgrounds and interests.

## Annotations

The annotations are brief and tell the reader what the story is about, and where and when it takes place. Teachers can quickly read the summaries and check off the books that interest them, or they can submit their choices to the local or school librarian and then decide if the text, style, illustrations, typography, and other characteristics are appropriate for their students.

Because institutional configurations and student interests and abilities vary considerably, I have avoided broad categories such as Elementary Level, Junior High School Level, and High School Level and, instead, suggested specific grade levels. The bibliography is arranged chronologically and reflects the social studies curricula used by most schools. If schools use a thematic approach, a quick reading of the annotations will allow teachers to mark in the margin those books that pertain to a specific theme, for example, (W) for war, (I) for immigration, etc.

For each entry, I have given the publisher and most recent date of publication. Where a significant discrepancy in dates exists, I have indicated the original publication date within brackets [ ].

Teachers might also find the following bibliographies helpful.

Abrahamson, Richard, and Betty Carter, eds. *Books for You: A Booklist for Senior High School Students.* Urbana, Ill.: National Council of Teachers of English (NCTE), 1988. NCTE publishes a new edition of this volume every five years. Although not limited to historical fiction, the editors group the titles according to subject or theme. They cite more than one thousand titles with short summaries.

Adamson, Lynda G. *A Reference Guide to Historical Fiction for Children and Young Adults.* New York: Greenwood Press, 1987. This book is arranged alphabetically by author and includes a lengthy discussion of these prolific authors and their works.

Howard, Elizabeth F. *America as Story: Historical Fiction for Secondary Schools.* Chicago: American Library Association, 1988. The author comments on and gives extensive summaries of 154 books. Most of the books, published within the last twenty years, focus on the experiences of average people who lived through important periods of U.S. history. A careful reading would help teachers develop thematic units.

"Notable Children's Trade Books in the Field of Social Studies" has appeared annually in *Social Education* since 1976. This annotated listing includes sections on a variety of topics in world history and culture and on American history, culture, and life among other important social studies topics.

*Subject Guide to Children's Books in Print 1988–1989.* R. R. Bowker. This guide, which covers books for children ages 3–18, includes more than six thousand subject headings and more than five thousand cross-references. It contains no annotations.

The bibliography has two major parts, United States History and World History.

## Coding for Special Topics

I have flagged books in the United States History section with a (●) if they relate to African Americans or (■) if they relate to Native Americans. I have not flagged books relating to Hispanic Americans and Asian Americans because those categories are too broad to be useful. Teachers seeking books about specific ethnic groups should read through the bibliography and choose those books that best meet their needs.

The following bibliographies, which specifically address multicultural issues, might also prove useful.

Hayden, Carla. *Venue into Cultures: A Resource Book of Multicultural Materials and Programs.* Chicago: American Library Association, 1991. The cultures represented include African-American, Arabic, Asian, Hispanic, Jewish, Native American, and Persian. The annotations cover picture books, fiction, folklore, and non-fiction.

Rudman, Marcia Kabakow. *Children's Literature: An Issues Approach.* New York: Longman Publishing Group, 1984. See chapter 5, "Heritage."

Sadker, Myra Pollack, and David Miller Sadker. *Now upon a Time.* New York: Harper and Row, 1977. See chapter 2, "The American Mosaic," which focuses on the portrayal of ethnic minorities in books.

Schwartz, Sheila. *Teaching Adolescent Literature.* Rochelle Park, N.J.: Hayden Books, 1979. See part 2, "Minorities," in which books are discussed in the context of group identity and pluralistic image versus the melting pot metaphor.

Tiedt, Pamela L., and Iris M. Tiedt. *Multicultural Teaching: A Handbook of Activities, Information, and Resources.* Boston: Allyn and Bacon, 1986. See chapter 9, "Reaching Out for More Information," which contains bibliographies for teachers and students.

Waldhorn, Arthur, Olga S. Weber, and Arthur Zeiger. *Good Reading.* R. R. Bowker, 1985. This book annotates over two thousand fiction and nonfiction titles for students age 13 and older. See the section "Regional and Cultural Minorities."

Williams, Helen E. *Books by African-American Authors and Illustrators.* Chicago: American Library Association, 1991. The author describes books appropriate for students in grades pre K–3, 5–8, and 9–up.

# United States History

## Settling America and Colonial Times

**Avi**
*Encounter at Easton*
Pantheon 1980
Grades 5–7
   Two indentured servants run away and try to start a new life.

**Avi**
*Night Journeys*
Pantheon 1979
Grades 5–9
   In the late 1700s two indentured servants escape to Pennsylvania.

**Baker, Betty**
■ *Walk the World's Rim*
Harper 1965
   In sixteenth century colonial Mexico a 14-year-old Indian boy becomes a member of deVaca's expedition through the southwest.

**Bulla, Clyde Robert**
*A Lion to Guard Us*
Crowell 1981
Grades 2–5
   Based on a true incident in 1609, the story recounts the adventures of three children who leave London and travel to the Virginia Colony to find their father.

**Bulla, Clyde Robert**
*Charlie's House*
Crowell 1983
Grades 2–5
   In the early 1700s an English boy is sent to the American colonies as an indentured servant.

**Clapp, Patricia**
*Constance: A Story of Early Plymouth*
Lothrop 1968
Grades 6–9
   A 15-year-old girl travels from London to Plymouth and settles down to colonial life.

**Cooper, James Fenimore**
*The Deerslayer*
Bantam 1982 [1841]
Grades 9–12
   The first of the Leatherstocking Tales is a wilderness adventure that takes place in the mid-1700s.

**Cooper, James Fenimore**
■ *Last of the Mohicans*
Bantam 1986 [1826]
Grades 9–12
   Indians are confronted with many problems caused by white settlers.

**Cross, Gilbert B.**
*A Witch across Time*
Atheneum 1990
Grades 6–9
   After being discharged from a treatment facility for anorexia, 15-year-old Hannah visits her aging aunt in Martha's Vineyard and is contacted by the ghost of Patience Cory who was hanged for witchcraft three hundred years ago. Through hypnosis Hannah becomes Patience and in alternating chapters the reader sees Hannah's search for evidence of Patience's existence and innocence and Patience's trial and execution.

**Dalgliesh, Alice**
■ *The Courage of Sarah Noble*
Scribners 1987 [1954]
Grades 3–5
   A girl accompanies her father to the Connecticut wilderness and finds out she has much in common with her Indian neighbors.

**de Angeli, Marguerite**
*Skippack School*
Doubleday 1961 [1939]
Grades 5–7

In 1750 a Mennonite boy proves his responsibility and is rewarded by his parents and teacher.

**Edmonds, Walter**
*The Matchlock Gun*
Dodd 1941
Grades 5–7

A boy protects his mother and sister from the Hudson Valley Indians.

**Edmonds, Walter**
*They Had a Horse*
Dodd 1962
Grades 6–8

In the early 1700s a 17-year-old boy and his 16-year-old bride struggle to buy a horse for their upstate New York farm.

**Farber, Norma**
■ *Mercy Short, A Winter Journal, North Boston, 1692–1693*
Dutton 1982
Grades 6–10

Based on a few lines in Cotton Mather's writings, this is the story of a girl who keeps a journal for a year in order to exorcise demons caused by her two-year captivity in an Indian village. Her memories are generally positive ones.

**Field, Rachel**
*Calico Bush*
Macmillan 1987 [1931]
Grades 5–9

A 13-year-old French girl, her grandmother, and uncle set sail for colonial America and when she is orphaned the girl becomes a bound-out servant to a family who is ill prepared for frontier life in Maine.

**Fleischman, Paul**
■ *Saturnalia*

Harper 1990
Grades 7–10

In 1681, six years after his Narraganset settlement was attacked and burned down, a Narraganset Indian boy who is apprenticed to a Boston printer searches for his twin brother and his heritage.

**Fletcher, Inglis**
*Lusty Wind for Carolina*
Queens House 1976 [1944]
Grades 10–12

A French Huguenot family settles in North Carolina where they plan to build a new life.

**Hawthorne, Nathaniel**
*The Scarlet Letter*
Dodd 1984 [1850]
Grades 7–12

Hester is forced to wear the letter "A" for adultery and face the anger and prejudice of the Puritan settlers in Massachusetts.

**Levitin, Sonia**
■ *Roanoke: A Novel of the Last Colony*
Atheneum 1973
Grades 6–8

An orphan leaves England for Chesapeake but ends up in Roanoke, Virginia, where he is befriended by Indians and eventually is saved by them.

**O'Dell, Scott**
● *My Name Is Not Angelica*
Houghton 1989
Grades 7–9

In 1733 a 16-year-old girl and a handsome tribal chief who are engaged to be married are captured and sold as slaves on the island of St. John. A revolt is organized and it ends in disaster.

**O'Dell, Scott**
*The Serpent Never Sleeps*
Houghton 1987
Grades 5–7

A 17-year-old girl leaves England for colonial America and after a shipwreck the survivors land in Jamestown, Virginia, where there is an extreme need for food.

**Petry, Ann**
● *Tituba of Salem Village*
Crowell 1964
Grades 7–9

Tituba and her husband are sold into slavery and end up in a Puritan home that is involved in witchcraft trials.

**Smith, Claude Clayton**
*The Stratford Devil*
Walker 1984
Grades 6–10

Based on a true incident in the 1600s the story concerns the adopted daughter of an elderly Connecticut widow accused of witchcraft.

**Speare, Elizabeth George**
■ *The Sign of the Beaver*
Houghton 1983
Grades 5–8

A boy is helped by an Indian boy to survive the harsh Maine wilderness winter.

**Speare, Elizabeth George**
*The Witch of Blackbird Pond*
Houghton 1958
Grades 6–9

A girl in Puritan Connecticut becomes friendly with an old woman who lives on the outskirts of the village and learns all about "guilt by association" when she and the old woman are accused of witchcraft.

**Starkey, Marion G.**
*The Visionary Girls: Witchcraft in Salem Village*
Little 1973
Grades 6–9

This is a fictionalized explanation of the Salem witch trials.

**Steele, William O.**
*Tomahawk Border*
Holt 1966
Grades 6–8

In 1714 a 16-year-old girl joins the Virginia Raiders.

**Steele, William O.**
■ *Wayah of the Real People*
Holt 1964
Grades 6–8

In 1750 a Cherokee boy goes to school in Williamsburg for one year and has difficulty adjusting to the new culture.

## American Revolution and the New Nation 1774–1779

**Anderson, Joan**
*1787*
Harcourt 1987
Grades 3–7

A boy sees the Constitution being written and comes to understand the effort and thought that went into the writing of this document.

**Avi**
*Captain Grey*
Pantheon 1977
Grades 6–8

In a secluded coastal town in New Jersey, just after the Revolution, an 11-year-old boy is held captive by a cruel man who sets up his own country.

**Avi**
*The Fighting Ground*
Lippincott 1984
Grades 7–9

A boy joins the army and must deal with his feelings about killing as well as his predicament as a prisoner of war.

**Beatty, John and Patricia**
*Who Comes to King's Mountain?*
Morrow 1975
Grades 6–8

A Scottish South Carolina boy has problems fighting with the rebels against the British.

**Berleth, Richard**
*Samuel's Choice*
Whitman 1990
Grades 4–6

In Brooklyn in 1779 a slave must decide whether to side with his master who is loyal to the English or offer his boating services to the revolutionary soldiers.

**Birnbaum, Louis**
*Red Dawn at Lexington*
Houghton 1986
Grades 9–12

This is an adventure story set against the Battle of Lexington.

**Boyd, James**
*Drums*
Scribner 1925
Grades 9–12

A teenage boy from North Carolina goes east to be educated, is sent to England on family business, returns home and joins the rebels, and gets to serve with John Paul Jones.

**Brady, Esther Wood**
*Tolliver's Secret*
Crown 1988
Grades 4–7

A girl carries a message for General Washington to a courier in British-held territory.

**Caudill, Rebecca**
*The Far-off Land*
Viking 1964
Grades 8–10

In 1780 a Moravian girl goes by flatboat from Salem to French Lick and has trouble accepting the hostile behavior toward Indians.

**Caudill, Rebecca**
*Tree of Freedom*
Viking 1949
Grades 7–9

Each child of a family moving to Kentucky may take one prized possession.

**Cavanna, Betty**
*Ruffles and Drums*
Morrow 1975
Grades 6–8

A patriotic girl nurses a wounded British officer and finds herself rethinking some of her beliefs.

**Clapp, Patricia**
*I'm Deborah Sampson: A Soldier of the
    American Revolution*
Lothrop 1977
Grades 6–8

A 10-year-old girl is bound-out to a good family and falls in love with one of the sons who is killed by the British. Disguised as a boy, she joins the Continental Army.

**Collier, Christopher and James Lincoln Collier**
*The Bloody Country*
Four Winds 1976
Grades 6–9

A family from Connecticut resettles in Pennsylvania and becomes enmeshed in a property conflict between the two states.

**Collier, James Lincoln**
● *Jump Ship to Freedom*
Delacorte 1981
Grades 4–6

A teenage slave escapes and tries to buy his and his mother's freedom.

Collier, Christopher and James Lincoln Collier
*My Brother Sam Is Dead*
Macmillan 1985 [1974]
Grades 6–9
   A family has divided loyalties during the Civil War.

Collier, Christopher and James Lincoln Collier
● *War Comes to Willy Freeman*
Delacorte 1983
Grades 4–6
   An African American girl sees her father die at the hands of the British and finds out that her mother was captured and taken to New York.

Collier, Christopher and James Lincoln Collier
*The Winter Hero*
Macmillan 1978
Grades 6–8
   A boy participates in Shay's Rebellion to protect farmers' property rights.

Collier, James Lincoln and Christopher Collier
● *Who Is Carrie?*
Delacorte 1984
Grades 4–6
   A slave girl searches for her origins.

Dalgliesh, Alice
*Adam and the Golden Cock*
Scribner 1959
Grades 3–5
   A boy is caught in a conflict of loyalties because his friend is from a Tory family.

Edmonds, Walter D.
*Drums along the Mohawk*
Bantam 1988 [1936]
Grades 9–12
   The novel tells the story of pioneer life in New York's Mohawk Valley during the Revolution.

Edwards, Sally
*George Midgett's War*
Scribner 1985

Grades 5–7
   A father and son supply the rebels and face dangers and conflicts in the process.

Fall, Thomas
● *Canalboat to Freedom*
Dial 1966
Grades 6–8
   An orphaned boy is indentured as a canalboat worker and becomes friends with a freed slave who awakens him to the horrors of slavery.

✓Fast, Howard
*April Morning*
Bantam 1981
Grades 7–10
   This is a fictionalized account of the Battle of Lexington.

Fast, Howard
*The Hessian*
Morrow 1972 [1961]
Grades 6–10
   Sixteen Hessian mercenaries and a drummer boy hang a retarded villager they suspect of spying and the villagers retaliate by killing all but the drummer boy. He escapes but is eventually found and tried.

Finlayson, Ann
*Rebecca's War*
Warne 1972
Grades 5–8
   British soldiers are billeted in Rebecca's Philadelphia home.

Fleischman, Paul
*Path of the Pale Horse*
Harper 1983
Grades 7–9
   A boy helps a doctor take care of yellow fever victims in the 1793 epidemic in Philadelphia.

Forbes, Esther
*Johnny Tremain*

Dell 1969 [1943]
Grades 6–9

An apprentice silversmith becomes involved in the patriots' cause.

**Forman, James**
*The Cow Neck Rebels*
Farrar 1969
Grades 9–12

Two brothers fight in the Battle of Long Island.

**Fritz, Jean**
*Early Thunder*
Putnam 1967
Grades 6–9

Just as the Revolutionary War is about to begin, the town of Salem finds its loyalties divided.

**Gauch, Patricia Lee**
*This Time Tempe Wick?*
Coward, McCann 1974
Grades 3–6

A girl outwits some disgruntled soldiers by hiding her horse in her bedroom.

**Green, Diana Huss**
*The Lonely War of William Pinto*
Little 1968
Grades 5–7

A Jewish boy in Connecticut cannot support the Revolution as do his father and brothers because of the vicious anti-Semitism of the time.

**Haynes, Betsy**
*Spies on the Devil's Belt*
Scholastic 1990
Grades 3–6

A 14-year-old boy joins the Continental army and becomes involved in a series of conspiracies.

**Hickman, Janet**
■ *The Valley of the Shadow*
Macmillan 1974
Grades 8–10

A 13-year-old Delaware Indian boy sees the events that ended in the massacre of 96 Moravian Indians by American militiamen.

**Holling, Holling C.**
*Tree in the Trail*
Houghton 1942
Grades 4–7

A 200-year-old cottonwood tree recounts the making of the Santa Fe Trail.

**Lawson, Robert**
*Ben and Me*
Little 1988 [1939]
Grades 4–6

A mouse helps Benjamin Franklin to succeed with his inventions and discoveries.

**Lawson, Robert**
*Mr. Revere and I*
Dell 1987
Grades 4–6

Paul Revere's adventures are told by his horse.

**Meadowcroft, Enid**
*By Wagon and Flatboat*
Harper 1938
Grades 5–7

A family travels by flatboat from Pennsylvania to Ohio.

**Monjo, F.N.**
*Grand Papa and Ellen Aroon*
Dell 1990 [1974]
Grades 4–6

Nine-year-old Ellen talks about times with her grandfather, Thomas Jefferson.

**Moore, Robin**
*The Bread Sister of Sinking Creek*
Lippincott 1990
Grades 5–8

In 1776 a 14-year-old girl travels with a pack-train from Philadelphia to the mountains in central Pennsylvania to join her aunt, only to find that her aunt moved to Ohio. She decides to stay and make a life for herself.

**O'Dell, Scott**
*Sarah Bishop*
Houghton 1980
Grades 5–8

The story, told in first person, depicts the pain, misery, and passion of the American Revolution.

**Pope, Elizabeth Marie**
*The Sherwood Ring*
Houghton 1958
Grades 8–10

This is a story of suspense filled with riddles that interlaces deftly romances of revolutionary times and today.

**Richter, Conrad**
■ *A Country of Strangers*
Schocken 1982 [1966]
Grades 6–8

A 15-year-old girl who was kidnapped at the age of five takes her son and flees from her Indian husband in the hope of finding her white family in Ohio. Her husband does not pursue her and her father refuses to accept her.

**Richter, Conrad**
■ *Light in the Forest*
Bantam 1984 [1953]
Grades 6–9

A boy who is captured and adopted by Indians is later returned to his parents and finds difficulty in reconciling the two worlds.

**Rinaldi, Ann**
*Time Enough for Dreams*
Holiday 1986
Grades 7–9

A girl is torn between her family's involvement in the fight for independence and her own feelings for a Tory sympathizer.

**Roberts, Kenneth**
*Arundel*
Fawcett 1981 [1933]
Grades 10–12

A Maine innkeeper is involved in the colonial fight for independence. Benedict Arnold is portrayed in a positive light as are the Native Americans.

**Roberts, Kenneth**
*Oliver Wiswell*
Doubleday 1952 [1940]
Grades 9–12

The story of the American Revolution is seen through the eyes of a young Bostonian who sided with the British.

**Roberts, Kenneth**
*Rabble in Arms*
Fawcett 1981 [1933]
Grades 9–12

Two brothers are scouts for Benedict Arnold.

**Steele, William O.**
*Buffalo Knife*
Odyssey 1990 [1952]
Grades 4–6

A 9-year-old boy has many adventures on a 1000 mile trip by flatboat.

**Steele, William O.**
*The Far Frontier*
Harcourt 1959
Grades 5–7

A boy is bound-out to an absent-minded scientist from Philadelphia who treks through the Tennessee wilderness.

**Steele, William O.**
*Flaming Arrows*
Odyssey 1990 [1957]
Grades 5–7

During pioneer days in Tennessee the town ostracizes the Logan family because Mr. Logan is a renegade fighting with the Indians.

Steele, William O.
■ *The Man with the Silver Eyes*
Harcourt 1976
Grades 5–7
   An Indian boy in Tennessee comes to admire a peace-loving white man.

Steele, William O.
■ *Tomahawks and Trouble*
Harcourt 1955
Grades 5–7
   Three children in Tennessee are captured by Indians. They escape, get lost in the woods, and find the situation worse than being captive.

Steele, William O.
*Trial through Danger*
Harcourt 1965
Grades 5–7
   A boy joins a hunting party in the Cherokee territory of North Carolina and is confronted by two fears—a fear of being massacred by the Indians and a fear of his companions finding out that his father had joined the Indians.

Steele, William O.
*Wilderness Journey*
Harcourt 1953
Grades 4–6
   A 10-year-old sickly boy who travels with a group of hunters becomes an independent pioneer.

Steele, William O.
*Winter Danger*
Odyssey 1990
Grades 5–7
   In 1780 a man leaves his son to grow up with a family in a Tennessee frontier village.

Vidal, Gore
*Burr*
Ballantine 1988 [1973]
Grades 11–12
   Told in the form of two memoirs, the novel recreates the story of the founding of the United States and the shortcomings of our founding fathers.

Wibberly, Leonard
*John Treegate's Musket*
Farrar 1959
Grades 7–9
   Defying his father's loyalties, a young boy fights against the British at Bunker Hill.

Wibberly, Leonard
*Peter Treegate's War*
Farrar 1960
Grades 7–9
   Peter is taken prisoner, escapes, crosses the Delaware with Washington, and goes to the southern mountains.

Wibberly, Leonard
*Sea Captain from Salem*
Farrar 1961
Grades 7–9
   Ben Franklin sends Peace of God Manly to France to find support for the Revolution.

Wibberly, Leonard
*Treegate's Raiders*
Farrar 1962
Grades 7–9
   Peter tries to recruit mountain men and has difficulty persuading Scottish settlers to forget their clan loyalties and feuds and unite as Americans.

## The Nation Expands and is Torn apart by War 1800–1860

Baker, Betty
■ *And One Was a Wooden Indian*
Macmillan 1970
Grades 8–10
   A young Apache follows a troop of white soldiers to retrieve a carving he believes put a curse on him.

**Baker, Betty**
*Do Not Annoy the Indians*
Macmillan 1968
Grades 6–8

A 13-year-old, his older sister, and younger brother go to Arizona from Philadelphia to join their father who runs the stagecoach station. They arrive to find that their father has gone to the gold fields and the boy takes over his duties.

**Baker, Betty**
*The Dunderhead War*
Harper 1967
Grades 6–8

In 1846 a 17-year-old boy travels with his uncle who is a volunteer in the war against Mexico.

**Beatty, Patricia**
■ *The Bad Bell of San Salvador*
Morrow 1973
Grades 5–8

In California a Comanche boy refuses to accept

the ways of his Mexican captors, but in spite of this he eventually wins their acceptance.

**Blos, Joan**
*Brothers of the Heart: A Story of the Old Northwest 1837–1838*
Macmillan 1987
Grades 6–10

A lame boy runs away after a quarrel with his father, finds work as a clerk in a fur trading company, and is left to spend the winter alone at the company cabin in the wilderness while his three companions travel on.

**Blos, Joan**
*A Gathering of Days: A New England Girl's Journal 1830–1832*
Sunburst 1979
Grades 6–9

In journal form a girl describes growing up in a New Hampshire town.

**Bohner, Charles**
*Bold Journey: West with Lewis and Clark*
Houghton 1985
Grades 6–10

This is a fictionalized account of the Corps of Discovery that highlights the part played by a boy.

**Bradley, David**
● *The Chaneysville Incident*
Avon 1981
Grades 10–12

A man returns to Pennsylvania to see his dying guardian and learns about his family's history and the resentments they harbored.

**Brady, Esther W.**
*The Toad on Capitol Hill*
Crown 1978
Grades 4–6

During the War of 1812 two boys find themselves in the way of oncoming British troops.

**Cheatham, Follis**
● *Bring Home the Ghost*
Harcourt 1980
Grades 9–12

The son of a slaveholder and his personal slave go west after fighting in a Seminole war. The reader can easily understand the difference between being treated as a free man and actually being free.

**Clark, Margaret Goff**
● *Freedom Crossing*
Scholastic 1989 [1969]
Grades 4–7

A Southern girl with Southern loyalties returns to her home up north and finds her father and brother helping runaway slaves.

**de Angeli, Marguerite**
*Whistle for the Crossing*
Doubleday 1977
Grades 4–6

In 1852 a boy goes with his train engineer

father on the first direct run from Philadelphia to Pittsburgh.

**De Felice, Cynthia**
*Weasel*
Macmillan 1990
Grades 6–9

An 11-year-old boy in 1839 Ohio finds his missing father caught and wounded in an animal trap and left for dead by a white Indian hunter.

**Forman, James**
● *So Ends This Day*
Farrar 1970
Grades 9–12

In the 1840s a 15-year-old boy goes with his father on a whaling ship to find his mother's killer and during the voyage learns that the ship is a slaver—not a whaler.

**Fox, Paula**
● *The Slave Dancer*
Bradbury 1973
Grades 6–9

A boy is kidnapped and impressed into service aboard an American slave ship which is going to Africa to pick up its cargo.

**Fritz, Jean**
● *Brady*
Puffin 1987 [1960]
Grades 4–7

Brady figures out that his minister father is involved in the underground railway and when his father is injured Brady helps in the evacuation of a slave boy.

**Griese, Arnold A.**
■ *The Way of Our People*
Crowell 1975
Grades 4–7

An Anvik Indian boy in Alaska who is afraid to hunt alone finds other ways to contribute to his tribe.

**Guthrie, A. B.**
*The Big Sky*
Houghton 1985 [1947]
Grades 7–12

In 1830 a boy runs away from the law and his abusive father to join a friend so that they can become mountain men.

**Haugaard, Kay**
*China Boy*
Abelard 1971
Grades 7–12

A 17-year-old Chinese immigrant comes to California to mine gold.

**Haynes, Betty**
● *Cowslip*
Nelson 1973
Grades 6–8

A 13-year-old slave girl lives among slaves who run away and becomes literate.

**Henry, Joanne Landers**
*Log Cabin in the Woods*
Four Winds 1988
Grades 4–6

This is the story of one year in the life of a pioneer boy.

**Highwater, Jamake**
■ *The Ceremony of Innocence*
Harper 1985
Grades 7–12

In the early 1800s a Blackfoot Indian tries to live in the white people's world—a world that will not condone her friendship with a French-Cree prostitute.

**Holland, Cecelia**
*The Bear Flag*
Houghton 1990
Grades 9–12

A young widow survives California frontier life and while participating in many historical events she interacts with notable people of the time.

**Holland, Isabelle**
*The Journey Home*
Scholastic 1990
Grades 4–7

Before their mother died she made arrangements for her two daughters to leave their New York City slum and be sent west to the Kansas prairie with a group of orphans looking for adoptive parents.

**Hotze, Sollace**
■ *A Circle Unbroken*
Clarion 1988
Grades 7–9

A girl finds it hard to adjust to her family after living nine years with the Dakota Sioux.

**Humphrey, William**
■ *No Resting Place*
Delacorte 1990
Grades 10–12

A father tells his son about the 1838–1839 Cherokee Trail of Tears holocaust.

**Hurmence, Belinda**
● *A Girl Called Boy*
Clarion 1982
Grades 6–8

A spoiled African-American girl is transported back to the days of slavery and tries to escape.

**Lampman, Evelyn Sibley**
■ *White Captives*
Atheneum 1975
Grades 5–6

A white man is a captive of the Apaches and then of the Mohaves.

**Lasky, Kathryn**
*Beyond the Divide*
Macmillan 1983
Grades 5–7

A girl runs away to join her father who has left for California. She gets lost in the Sierra Nevada and has to survive.

**Lenski, Lois**
*Prairie School*
Lippincott 1951
Grades 4–7

A South Dakota family survives the Great Blizzard of 1849.

**Levitin, Sonia**
*The No-Return Trail*
Harcourt 1978
Grades 5–7

A 17-year-old who is both wife and mother joins an 1841 wagon train.

**Loeper, John J.**
*The Golden Dragon*
Atheneum 1978
Grades 5–6

In the mid 1800s a clipper ship sails from New York to San Francisco.

**Longworth, Polly**
● *I, Charlotte Forten, Black and Free*
Crowell 1970
Grades 5–7

This fictionalized biography tells about a woman's fight for equal rights and also includes the work of abolitionists such as Frederick Douglass and William Wells Brown.

**Lord, Athena V.**
*A Spirit to Ride the Whirlwind*
Macmillan 1981
Grades 6–9

In 1836 a 12-year-old works in a mill in Lowell, Massachusetts.

**MacLachlan, Patricia**
*Sarah Plain and Tall*
Harper 1985
Grades 3–6

After their mother dies, two prairie children are to have a new mother who is a mail-order bride.

**McClung, Robert M.**
*Hugh Glass, Mountain Man*
Morrow 1990
Grades 5–8

This is a fictionalized account of a man who was mauled by a grizzly bear and left to die. He managed a 200-mile crawl through the wilderness to reach a settlement.

**McGraw, Eloise**
■ *Moccasin Trail*
Coward 1952
Grades 7–9

A white boy is attacked by a bear, rescued, and raised by Crow Indians. He has many conflicts when he is reunited with his family.

**Moore, Ruth Nulton**
*Wilderness Journey*
Herald 1979
Grades 6–8

Two Irish boys journey through rugged terrain as they set out from Philadelphia to join their mother in Pittsburgh.

**Morrow, Honore**
*On to Oregon!*
Morrow 1976 [1925]
Grades 5–9

In 1848 the Sager children travel from Missouri to Oregon by covered wagon.

**Morrow, Lisa Ketchum**
*West against the Wind*
Holiday 1987
Grades 4–6

A 14-year-old girl, her mother, and brother go by wagon train to California to join the children's father who is working in the gold fields.

**Oates, Stephen B.**
● *The Fires of Jubilee*
New American Library 1982 [1975]
Grades 7–9

This is a fictionalized account of Nat Turner's rebellion.

**O'Dell, Scott**
*The Dark Canoe*
Houghton 1968
Grades 9–12

Three brothers sail from Nantucket to find out what happened to the ship, *Amy Foster*.

**O'Dell, Scott**
● *Island of the Blue Dolphins*
Dell 1989 [1960]
Grades 7–9

Before her rescue, an Alaskan Indian girl spends eighteen years alone on a Pacific island.

**O'Dell, Scott**
● *Streams to the River, River to the Sea*
Houghton 1986
Grades 7–9

Sacagawea, abducted by the Minnetarees, marries a French trader and accompanies Lewis and Clark on their expedition.

**Parker, F. M.**
*The Far Battleground*
Signet 1988
Grades 7–9

Based on a true incident, the novel concerns the confrontation of two officers during the Mexican War.

**Parker, F. M.**
*The Searchers*
Signet 1986
Grades 7–12

A 16-year-old boy and his sister are orphaned after a Comanche raid and are kidnapped and sold as slaves in Mexico. The boy escapes and searches for his sister.

**Putnam, Alice**
*Westering*
Lodestar 1990
Grades 4–6

A boy and his dog ride the wagon train to Oregon.

**Speare, Elizabeth George**
■ *Calico Captive*
Dell 1989 [1957]
Grades 4–6

Based on an incident in 1807, this is the story of a girl taken captive in an Indian raid and forced to march to Montreal, Canada, where she is sold to the French.

**St. George**
*The Halo Wind*
Putnam 1978
Grades 5–7

A 13-year-old girl on a wagon trip to Oregon notices the luck of the wagon train changes for the worse when they take on a Chinook Indian girl.

**Steele, William O.**
*The Lone Hunt*
Harcourt 1976 [1956]
Grades 5–7

A boy from Tennessee hunts for the last buffalo in the Cumberland Mountains.

**Steele, William O.**
■ *The War Party*
Harcourt 1978
Grades 4–6

A young brave comes to understand the inhumanity and brutality of war when he is wounded during his first war party.

**Taylor, Theodore**
*Walking up a Rainbow*
Dell 1988
Grades 7–9

In the 1850s an orphaned girl is left with 2,000 sheep and an enormous debt. She starts her own wagon train to Sacramento where she plans to sell the sheep to gold miners.

**Vining, Elizabeth Gray**
*The Taken Girl*
Hall 1973
Grades 8–10

An orphaned servant girl in pre-Civil War Philadelphia works in the abolitionist movement with John Greenleaf Whittier.

**Wallin, Luke**
■ *In the Shadow of the Wind*
Bradbury 1984
Grades 6–10

Tensions exist between white settlers and Creek Indians in 1830s Alabama that eventually lead to the removal of the Creeks to Oklahoma.

**Welch, James**
■ *Fools Crow*
Penguin 1987
Grades 7–12

An 18-year-old Blackfoot Indian in Montana tries to make his people understand the whites who are menacing Indian customs and traditions.

**West, Jessamyn**
■ *The Massacre at Fall Creek*
Harcourt 1975
Grades 7–12

This is a fictionalized account of an 1824 incident in Indiana where five white men killed nine innocent and peaceful Seneca Indians. Threatened by reprisals, the United States government agreed to try the men for murder.

**Whelan, Gloria**
■ *Next Spring an Oriole*
Random 1987
Grades 3–5

In 1837 new settlers on the Michigan frontier aid a sick Indian girl and their good deed is repaid by the Indians.

**Wibberly, Leonard**
*Red Pawns*
Farrar 1973

Grades 6–8

The story concerns the War of 1812.

**Winter, Jeanette**
● *Follow the Drinking Gourd*
Knopf 1988
Grades 2–5

A conductor on the underground railroad taught slaves the words to the song "Follow the Drinking Gourd" which was, in reality, a map to freedom in Canada. The reader follows the map through the depiction of one family.

**Wisler, Clifton**
■ *Buffalo Moon*
Lodestar 1984
Grades 6–8

A 14-year-old boy leaves his Texas ranch and stays with the Comanche Indians for six months to avoid being sent to school in New Orleans.

**Wisler, Clifton**
*Piper's Ferry*
Lodestar 1990
Grades 5–8

This is a fictionalized account of Texas's struggle for independence.

**Wisler, Clifton**
■ *Winter of the Wolf*
Nelson 1981
Grades 6–10

A 14-year-old boy saves the life of a Comanche boy. They become friends and hunt for a silver wolf who is thought to be a devil.

**Wisler, Clifton**
■ *Wolf's Tooth*
Lodestar 1987
Grades 6–8

A white boy and an Indian boy share friendship, adventure, and hardship on the 1827 frontier.

## Civil War and Reconstruction 1861–1865

**Beatty, Patricia**
*Blue Stars Watching*
Morrow 1969
Grades 5–7

Although a 13-year-old is sent from Delaware to California with his sister to avoid the dangers of the Civil War, he manages to get mixed up with Rebel plotters and Union spies.

**Beatty, Patricia**
*Charley Skedaddle*
Morrow 1987
Grades 4–7

A 12-year-old enlists as a drummer boy both for excitement and to avenge his brother's death. When confronted with the realities of war, he runs away because he is frightened.

**Beatty, Patricia and Phillip Robins**
*Eben Tyne, Powdermonkey*
Morrow 1990
Grades 5–8

Eben Tyne, a gunpowder carrier for the Confederate *Merrimack*, is involved in the battle with the USS *Monitor* and it changes his life.

**Beatty, Patricia**
*Turn Homeward, Hannalee*
Morrow 1984
Grades 6–8

A 12-year-old girl is sent north to work in a Yankee mill and tries to return to her family in Georgia.

**Beatty, Patricia**
■ *Wait for Me, Watch for Me, Eula Bee*
Morrow 1978
Grades 6–8

In 1861 two children are captured by Comanche Indians in Texas.

**Braun, Matt**
● *Black Fox*
Signet 1988
Grades 7–9
After a surprise raid by the Comanches, an ex-slave frees the people of a Texas town.

**Brink, Carol Ryrie**
*Caddie Woodlawn*
Macmillan 1973
Grades 4–6
In 1864 an 11-year-old tomboy has many adventures while growing up on the Wisconsin frontier.

**Brown, Rita Maerie**
*High Hearts*
Bantam 1986
Grades 9–12
An 18-year-old girl disguised as a boy joins the First Virginia Cavalry so she can be with her husband.

**Clapp, Patricia**
*The Tamarack Tree: A Novel of the Siege of Vicksburg*
Penguin 1988
Grades 7–10
A British girl experiences the siege of Vicksburg.

**Climo, Shirley**
*A Month of Seven Days*
Crowell 1987
Grades 5–7
Zoe's job is to scare away the Yankee soldiers who have taken over her Georgia home.

**Crane, Stephen**
*The Red Badge of Courage*
Penguin 1987 [1895]
Grades 9–12
This is a graphic, unforgettable account of a young Union soldier's shattering Civil War experiences.

**Cummings, Betty Sue**
*Hew against the Grain*
Atheneum 1977
Grades 6–9
A 15-year-old girl tells the story of her divided family in the middle of the ruin and devastation of war-torn Virginia.

**Fast, Howard**
● *Freedom Road*
Amsco 1970 [1944]
Grades 6–9
An ex-slave and a Union soldier return to South Carolina and find a new kind of tyranny.

**Forkner, Ben and Patrick Samway (eds.)**
● *Stories of the Old South*
Penguin 1986
Grades 9–12
The stories are paired with the commentary of modern writers and the result is a stunning portrayal of the South from antebellum times to Reconstruction.

**Freedman, Florence**
● *Two Tickets to Freedom*
Simon and Schuster 1971
Grades 4–6
A boy and a girl escape from slavery and go to England. After the Civil War they return and start a school for rural African-American children.

**Gauch, Patricia Lee**
*Thunder at Gettysburg*
Putnam 1990 [1975]
Grades 3–6
Without planning to do so, a 14-year-old girl becomes part of the battle.

**Gessner, Lynne**
■ *Navajo Slave*
Harvey House 1976
Grades 5–7
After the Civil War a Navajo boy escapes from slavery in New Mexico.

**Hamilton, Virginia**
■ *The Magical Adventures of Pretty Pearl*
Harper 1983
Grades 7–9

During Reconstruction times in Georgia an African godchild comes to the New World and connects with a secret community of blacks who are to establish contact with a Cherokee band.

**Hansen, Joyce**
● *Which Way Freedom*
Walker 1986
Grades 6–8

A former slave serves with the Union army.

**Haugaard, Erik**
*Orphans of the Wind*
Houghton 1966
Grades 7–9

A 12-year-old boy sails from Bristol as a deckhand on a blockade runner.

**Hickman, Janet**
*Zoar Blue*
Macmillan 1978
Grades 6–9

A young girl who is part of a pacifist community feels the effects of war.

**Hunt, Irene**
*Across Five Aprils*
Ace 1964
Grades 6–9

A family living in the border state of Illinois is divided in loyalties and joins opposing armies.

**Hurmence, Belinda**
● *Tancy*
Clarion 1984
Grades 3–6

When the Civil War ends a young girl who is a house slave leaves North Carolina to search for her mother who was sold when the girl was a baby.

**Jones, Douglas C.**
*Elkhorn Tavern*
Holt 1980
Grades 9–12

A woman and her two children are left behind on their Arkansas farm when her husband leaves to fight the Yankees.

**Jones, Douglas C.**
*Roman*
Holt 1986
Grades 9–12

After the Civil War an 18-year-old boy is on his own in the wild west.

**Kantor, McKinlay**
*Andersonville*
Signet 1957
Grades 10–12

Andersonville, the Confederate prison meant to hold 10,000 men, eventually housed more than 30,000 Yankee soldiers at one time.

**Keith, Harold**
■ *Rifles for Watie*
Crowell 1957
Grades 7–9

A farm boy joins the Union army, is sent west, and becomes a scout with Stand Watie's Cherokee rebels.

**Lester, Julius**
● *This Strange New Feeling*
Scholastic 1985
Grades 6–12

This is a collection of three love stories based on slave narratives.

**Mitchell, Margaret**
*Gone with the Wind*
Avon 1986 [1936]
Grades 10–12

A love story set in war-torn Atlanta paints a vivid picture of the times and the issues of the Civil War.

**Morrison, Toni**
● *Beloved*
Knopf 1987
Grades 9–12
By way of the memories and voices of different characters the reader experiences slavery.

**O'Dell, Scott**
*The 290*
Houghton 1976
Grades 6–8
A boy signs on as a sailor on the *Alabama*, a ship he helped build in England. He experiences many battles, including an attempted mutiny and an effort to free slaves being held in Haiti.

**O'Dell, Scott**
■ *Sing down the Moon*
Houghton 1970
Grades 5–8
A Navajo girl tells of the 1864 forced march to Fort Sumner.

**Perez, N. A.**
*The Slopes of War*
Houghton 1984
Grades 7–9
Two cousins fight each other at Gettysburg.

**Reeder, Carolyn**
*Shades of Gray*
Macmillan 1989
Grades 5–8
A 12-year-old orphan boy goes to live with his aunt's family in post-Civil War Virginia and comes to understand his uncle's refusal to fight.

**Rinaldi, Ann**
*The Last Silk Dress*
Holiday 1988
Grades 7–9
A girl helps the Confederates and uncovers family secrets.

**Sebestyen, Ouida**
● *Words by Heart*
Bantam 1983
Grades 5–7
During Reconstruction an African-American family moves into an all-white community.

**Shaara, Michael**
*The Killer Angels*
Ballantine 1974
Grades 9–12
The story focuses on Gettysburg during the four bloodiest days of the battle.

**Shore, Lara Jan**
*The Sacred Moon Tree*
Bradbury 1986
Grades 6–10
Two youngsters experience the Civil War differently.

**Smucker, Barbara**
● *Runaway to Freedom: A Story of the Underground Railway*
Harper 1978
Grades 4–8
Two 12-year-old slave girls escape from the South and try to reach Canada and freedom.

**Sneve, Virginia**
■ *Betrayed*
Holiday 1974
Grades 5–7
This novel is a painful and cruel account of white-Indian conflicts during the Civil War.

**Steele, William O.**
*The Perilous Road*
Odyssey 1990 [1958]
Grades 5–7
A Tennessee mountain boy who hates Yankees learns about the fruitlessness of war.

**Stone, Irving**
*The President's Lady*

Signet 1968 [1951]
Grades 9–12

Based on historical fact the novel shows how Jackson's love for Rachel influenced United States history.

**Turner, Ann**
● *Nettie's Trip South*
Macmillan 1987
Grades 2–5

Nettie writes to her friend after a trip to the Civil War South and describes vividly the realities of slavery.

**Walker, Margaret**
● *Jubilee*
Bantam 1975 [1966]
Grades 9–12

Through the eyes of a young slave girl the reader sees the Civil War and Reconstruction.

**Wicker, Tom**
*Unto This Hour*
Viking 1984
Grades 9–12

Seen from two points of view, North and South, the story graphically depicts the Battle of Bull Run.

**Winter, Jeanette**
● *Follow the Drinking Gourd*
Knopf 1989
Grades 3–5

Based on the lyrics of a slave song, a legendary sailor directs runaway slaves to freedom.

**Wisler, Clifton**
*Thunder on the Tennessee*
Dutton 1983
Grades 6–9

A boy joins the Confederate army and sees for himself the abomination of war.

## The Transformation of a Nation 1866–1899

**Aldrich, Bess Streeter**
*A Lantern in Her Hand*
Signet 1983 [1928]
Grades 7–9

A woman leaves Iowa for the Nebraska frontier with her Civil War veteran husband and young child.

**Aldrich, Bess**
*Song of Years*
Signet 1985 [1939]
Grades 7–9

A young woman grows from childhood to adulthood on the Iowa prairie.

**Alexander, Lloyd**
*The Philadelphia Adventure*
Dutton 1990
Grades 5–8

During the 1876 Philadelphia Centennial Exhibition the Emperor of Brazil's grandchildren are kidnapped and Vesper Holly responds to an appeal for help from President Grant.

**Anderson, Sherwood**
*Winesburg, Ohio*
Penguin 1988 [1919]
Grades 10–12

The novel presents a picture of small town life in Middle America during the 1800s.

**Arnold, Elliot**
■ *The Camp Grant Massacre*
Simon and Schuster 1976
Grades 9–12

This is a fictionalized account of the massacre of an unarmed Apache tribe in Arizona.

**Avi**
*Emily Upham's Revenge*
Pantheon 1978

Grades 4–6

In 1875 Massachusetts a 7-year-old girl is sent to live with her rich uncle and becomes involved in a suspicious bank robbery.

Baker, Betty
*The Night Spider Case*
Macmillan 1984
Grades 4–6

In New York City in the 1890s an 11-year-old boy teams up with a friend to investigate an empty house.

Baker, Betty
*The Spirit is Willing*
Morrow 1974
Grades 8–10

A girl in an Arizona mining town in the 1800s

refuses to accept the town's attitude about girls not being able to do exciting things.

Beatty, Patricia
*By Crumbs, It's Mine!*
Morrow 1976
Grades 6–8

After being stranded in the Arizona Territory a girl finds herself owner of a traveling hotel.

Beatty, Patricia
*Hail Columbia*
Morrow 1970
Grades 6–8

In 1893 Oregon a suffragette incites the town.

Beatty, Patricia
*How Many Miles to Sundown?*
Morrow 1974
Grades 7–9

In 1881 a girl, her brother, and her pet longhorn go with a 15-year-old boy to Texas, New Mexico, and Arizona to help him find his father.

Beatty, Patricia
*Just Some Weeds from the Wilderness*

Morrow 1978
Grades 7–9

A girl's aunt goes into the patent medicine business in Oregon.

Beatty, Patricia
*Me, California Perkins*
Morrow 1968
Grades 5–7

In 1882 a family lives in a town in the Mojave Desert.

Beatty, Patricia
*Melinda Takes A Hand*
Morrow 1983
Grades 7–9

In 1893 a 13-year-old girl is stranded in a Colorado town and quickly becomes a part of it.

Beatty, Patricia
*The Nickel-Plated Beauty*
Morrow 1964
Grades 4–6

In 1886 in the Washington Territory, a 12-year-old girl, her 13-year-old brother, and five younger children manage to get a new kitchen stove to replace the rusted-out one.

Beatty, Patricia
*The Queen's Own Grove*
Morrow 1966
Grades 4–5

In 1887 a proper English family migrates to California to restore the health of the father and there they plant an orange grove.

Beatty Patricia
*Red Rock over the River*
Morrow 1973
Grades 7–9

In 1881 at Fort Yuma in Arizona a girl becomes involved in a prison escape.

Beatty, Patricia
*Something to Shout About*

Morrow 1976

Grades 6–8

Based on fact, this story concerns a woman's fundraising drive for a new schoolhouse in a gold mining town in Montana Territory.

**Beatty, Patricia**
*That's One Ornery Orphan*
Morrow 1980
Grades 4–6

A 13-year-old girl is sent to an orphanage and is taken into a number of foster homes where she is overworked and mistreated.

**Benchley, Nathaniel**
■ *Only Earth and Sky Last Forever*
Harper 1972
Grades 7–9

A young Sioux Indian fights at the Battle of Little Big Horn.

**Berger, Thomas**
■ *Little Big Man*
Dell 1985 [1964]
Grades 10–12

A 111-year-old man, the son of two fathers— one white and the other a Cheyenne chief—tells the story of his life.

**Braun, Matt**
*The Brannocks*
Signet 1986
Grades 7–10

Just after the Civil War three brothers are reunited in Denver, which has become a boom town.

**Braun, Matt**
*Windward West*
Signet 1987
Grades 7–10

The three brothers settle in different parts of the country. One becomes a railroad baron, the second an army scout, and the third a renegade Indian trader.

**Braun, Matt**
*Rio Hondo*
Signet 1987
Grades 7–10

The three brothers reunite and try to clean up the New Mexico Territory by getting rid of cattle rustlers and dishonest politicians.

**Braun, Matt**
*A Distant Land*
Signet 1988
Grades 7–10

Clint Brannock, a Deputy U.S. Marshal, hunts down the leader of an outlaw band trying to force land reform.

**Brown, Dee**
■ *Creek Mary's Blood*
Holt 1980
Grades 10–12

A half-Creek, half-Cherokee boy who has lived most of his life with the Cheyennes retells his life story to a reporter when he is ninety-one.

**Burchard, Peter**
*Digger: A Novel*
Putnam 1980
Grades 6–9

A newsboy has many adventures in New York City in 1871.

**Calvert, Patricia**
*The Snowbird*
Scribner 1980
Grades 9–12

In 1883 two orphaned Tennessee children are sent west to live with relatives in the Dakota Territory.

**Carter, Peter**
*Borderlands*
Farrar 1990
Grades 7–10

In 1871 two brothers join a cattle drive to California where the older brother is shot by gamblers. The younger seeks revenge and in the ensuing years, becomes successful, moves to Dodge, opens a store, flees in the 1873 financial panic—and then meets his nemesis.

**Cather, Willa**
■ *Death Comes for the Archbishop*
Vintage 1971 [1927]
Grades 9–12
When the diocese of New Mexico is established it affects the Navajo and Hopi Indians.

**Clark, Walter van Tilburg**
*The Ox-Bow Incident*
Signet 1943
Grades 7–12
Frontier justice in 1880 Nevada leads to unfortunate results.

**Conrad, Pam**
*My Daniel*
Harper 1989
Grades 5–7
A woman tells her grandchildren about how her brother was destroyed during the hunt for dinosaur remains in Nebraska.

**Cummings, Betty Sue**
*Now, Ameriky*
Atheneum 1979
Grades 5–8
A young Irish girl comes to the United States to find work and bring over the rest of her family.

**de Angeli, Marguerite**
*Fiddlestrings*
Doubleday 1974
Grades 5–7
In 1898 an 11-year-old boy learns that practicing his violin is worth his while.

**Dreiser, Theodore**
*Sister Carrie*

Penguin 1981 [1932]
Grades 10–12
In 1889 an 18-year-old girl comes to Chicago from the Midwest to make her fortune.

**Dunbar, Laurence**
● *The Sport of Gods*
Dodd 1981
Grades 10–12
In the mid 1890s an African-American family moves from the South to New York City and must cope with the problems of urban life.

**Fleming, Alice**
*The King of Prussia and a Peanut Butter Sandwich*
Scribner 1988
Grades 4–6
The Prussian Mennonites immigrated to the Crimea in Russia where they were given one hundred years of freedom from military service. There they learned about winter wheat and when they came to Kansas they planted it instead of corn.

**Garland, Hamlin**
*Main-Travelled Roads*
Signet 1962
Grades 7–12
The short stories deal with Midwest farm life.

**Gregory, Kristiana**
■ *Jenny of the Tetons*
Harcourt 1989
Grades 5–7
A little girl's parents die in an Indian raid and she goes to live with an English trapper, his Indian wife, and six children.

**Griese, Arnold**
■ *At the Mouth of the Luckiest River*
Crowell 1973
Grades 3–5
In 1873 an Athabascan Indian boy opposes the medicine man in order to avoid problems with the Eskimos.

**Guthrie, A. A.**
*The Way West*
Houghton 1949
Grades 10–12

This Pulitzer Prize-winning novel draws a good picture of wagon train life showing how the wagon gets started, how people are found to go, how the train is governed, and then the journey itself to Oregon.

**Hall, Lynn**
*Gently Touch the Milkweed*
Follett 1970
Grades 6–10

A girl works at her parents' inn on the wagon train route to Kansas.

**Harvey, Brett**
*Cassie's Journey: Going West in the 1860s*
Holiday 1988
Grades 4–6

Based on women's diaries the novel presents a good picture of daily hardships faced by people on the wagon train.

**Highwater, Jamake**
■ *Eyes of Darkness*
Lothrop 1985
Grades 6–9

A young Indian boy is taken from his home and sent east to become a doctor. When he returns home he tries to help his people see the best of two worlds—but neither world wants him.

**Highwater, Jamake**
■ *I Wear the Morning Star*
Harper 1986
Grades 7–9

Sitko is placed in an orphanage by his mother but holds fast to his Indian heritage.

**Highwater, Jamake**
■ *Legend Days*
Harper 1984
Grades 7–9

An Indian girl tries to hold on to her heritage as she sees the civilization she loves crumble around her because of sickness, hunger, and the continual invasion of white settlers.

**Hudson, Jan**
■ *Sweetgrass*
Philomel 1989
Grades 6–8

A 15-year-old Blackfoot Indian girl saves her family from a smallpox epidemic.

**Jackson, Helen Hunt**
■ *Ramona*
Signet 1939
Grades 7–12

This is a fictionalized account of the Native Americans' fight for survival and the importance of blood ties, religion, and the uses of power.

**Jones, Douglas C.**
■ *Arrest Sitting Bull*
Scribner 1977
Grades 10–12

A woman teacher at Standing Rock Agency is caught up in a struggle between the Sioux and the whites.

**Jones, Douglas C.**
■ *The Court-Martial of George Armstrong Custer*
Scribner 1976
Grades 9–12

Through witnesses for the defense and prosecution, the Battle of Little Big Horn is brought to life.

**Jones, Douglas C.**
■ *Gone the Dreams and Dancing*
Holt 1987
Grades 9–12

A Comanche chief negotiates with his white victors and tries to effect a bargain that will permit his people to keep their identity and self-respect.

**Jones, Douglas C.**
*Remember Santiago*
Holt 1988
Grades 9–12

The United States Army in Cuba proves to be uncontrolled and poorly trained.

**Keith, Harold**
*The Obstinate Land*
Crowell 1977
Grades 10–12

In 1893 a 14-year-old boy assumes responsibility for his family when his father freezes to death on their pioneer farm in the Cherokee Strip of Oklahoma.

**L'Amour, Louis**
*Bendigo Shafter*
Bantam 1983
Grades 9–12

With great difficulty and arduous work, people overcome obstacles to build a town in Indian territory.

**Lane, Rose Wilder**
*Young Pioneers*
McGraw 1976
Grades 6–8

A young couple homesteads in the Dakota Territory. With the grasshopper infestation the man is forced to go back east to earn money and the woman and newborn baby remain behind and brave the frontier disasters.

**Lasky, Kathryn**
*The Bone Wars*
Puffin 1989
Grades 5–9

Two boys are caught in the middle of the warring bone hunters in the Montana Badlands.

**Lawson, Laurie**
*Addie across the Prairie*
Whitman 1986
Grades 3–6

A 9-year-old crosses the prairie with her family to start a new life in the Dakota Territory.

**Lawlor, Laurie**
*Addie's Dakota Winter*
Whitman 1989
Grades 4–6

A 10-year-old girl and her 9-year-old brother go to school in the Dakota Territory of 1883 and learn about prejudice against immigrants as well as a host of other lessons not found in school books.

**Levin, Betty**
*Brother Moose*
Greenwillow 1990
Grades 5–8

In the late 1800s unwanted children in England were shipped to foster parents in Canada. In this story two youngsters survive a series of hardships and end up in Maine.

**Magnuson, James and Dorethea G. Petrie**
*Orphan Train*
Dial 1978
Grades 9–12

A woman travels by train with twenty-seven New York City street children to find adoptive homes for them in the Midwest.

**Mayne, William**
■ *Drift*
Hall 1986
Grades 6–9

Lost in the forest, Rafe is a captive of two Indian women who teach him to live off the land.

**McClain, Margaret S.**
*Bellboy: A Mule Train Journey*
New Mexico Press 1989
Grades 6–8

In the Northwest California Territory in the 1870s a 12-year-old boy takes a job as a bellboy to help support his family and rides the lead animal in a mule train.

**McMurty, Larry**
*Lonesome Dove*
Dial 1985
Grades 9–12
    Using the vehicle of a cattle drive, the author epitomizes the American western experience.

**Moeri, Louise**
*Save Queen of Sheba*
Dutton 1981
Grades 5–7
    There is a wagon train massacre and a boy must take care of his younger sister.

**Nixon, Jean Lowery**
*[Four books in the Orphan Train Quartet]*
*A Family Apart*
Bantam 1988
Grades 4–6
    A 13-year-old girl, the oldest of six, has been sent west on the Orphan Train to find adoptive parents for herself and her five siblings.

———
*Caught in the Act*
Bantam 1988
Grades 5–7
    Mike is adopted by German immigrants in Missouri.

———
*In the Face of Danger*
Bantam 1989
Grades 5–7
    Megan is adopted and goes to live in the rugged Kansas Territory.

———
*A Place to Belong*
Bantam 1989
Grades 5–7
    Danny and Peg are adopted by a nice couple from St. Louis, Missouri.

**O'Dell, Scott**
■ *Zia*
Houghton 1976
Grades 7–9
    The sequel to *Island of the Blue Dolphins* tells the story of what happened to Karana after she was brought to the California mission.

**Parker, F. M.**
*The Predators*
New American Library 1990
Grades 9–12
    This is a fictional account of the Mormons who tried to establish a polygamous nation by crossing the country and establishing roots in Utah.

**Rappaport, Doreen**
*Trouble at the Mines*
Bantam 1989
Grades 4–7
    The story tells of family ties that are destroyed by the 1899 Pennsylvania coal miners' strike. Mother Jones, the union organizer, figures largely in the story.

**Rockwood, Joyce**
■ *To Spoil the Sun*
Holt 1987
Grades 8–10
    A Cherokee girl tells about village life before and after the devastation caused by a smallpox epidemic.

**Rolvaag, O. E.**
*Giants in the Earth*
Harper 1965 [1929]
Grades 9–12
    Norwegian immigrants barely eke out a living on the Dakota plains.

**Talbot, Charlene Joy**
*The Sodbuster Adventure*
Atheneum 1982
Grades 6–8
    When her fiancé dies, a young woman and a 13-year-old girl work his mining claim in Kansas.

**Turner, Ann**
*Grasshopper Summer*
Macmillan 1989
Grades 5–7
   In 1874 a boy and his family travel from Kentucky to the Dakota Territory.

**Twain, Mark**
● *The Adventures of Huckleberry Finn*
Harper 1965 [1884]
Grades 9–12
   This is a story about adventures on and around the Mississippi River on which Huck travels with a runaway slave.

**Uchida, Yoshiko**
*Samurai of the Gold Hill*
Scribner 1972
Grades 5–7
   In 1869 Japanese immigrants come to California.

**Wilder, Laura Ingalls**
*[Series of nine Little House books]*
*Little House in the Big Woods*
Harper 1953 [1932]
Grades 3–7
   The first book in the series deals with life in a Wisconsin log house.

———
*Little House on the Prairie*
Harper 1953 [1935]
Grades 3–7
   The Ingalls family moves west in a covered wagon.

———
*Farmer Boy*
Harper 1953 [1933]
Grades 3–7
   This is the story of Alonzo Wilder's youth on a farm in upstate New York.

———
*On the Banks of Plum Creek*
Harper 1953 [1937]
Grades 3–7
   The Ingalls family face many hardships after moving to Minnesota.

———
*By the Shores of Silver Lake*
Harper 1953 [1939]
Grades 4–8
   The family moves to the Dakota Territory and Laura's father works in a railroad building camp.

———
*The Long Winter*
Harper 1953 [1940]
Grades 4–8
   During the 1880–1881 winter the village was on the edge of starvation.

———
*Little Town on the Prairie*
Harper 1953 [1941]
Grades 4–8
   At the age of 15, Laura receives her teaching certificate.

———
*These Happy Golden Years*
Harper 1953 [1943]
Grades 5–9
   Laura and Alonzo marry, file a homestead claim, and move into their own home.

———
*The First Four Years*
Harper 1971
Grades 5–9
   The Wilders homestead in Dakota and their daughter is born.

**Yee, Paul**
*Tales from the Gold Mountain*
Macmillan 1990
Grades 4–8

The stories in this collection deal with Chinese immigrants in the United States—their successes, failures, and adventures.

**Young, Alida E.**
*Land of the Iron Dragon*
Doubleday 1978
Grades 6–9

In 1865 a young boy finds work with thousands of other Chinese on the transcontinental railroad.

---

## World War I and the Great Depression 1900–1939

**Aaron, Chester**
*Lackawanna*
Lippincott 1986
Grades 7–9

This is a Depression story in which an abandoned boy and five other children set up housekeeping in a tin shack and learn how to survive.

**Angell, Judie**
*One-way to Ansonia*
Bradbury 1985
Grades 7–10

In the early 1900s Rose and her siblings emigrate from Russia to crowded New York City.

**Armer, Laura A.**
■ *Waterless Mountain*
McKay 1959 [1931]
Grades 5–7

A Navajo boy who lives on the edge of the white man's world is constantly reminded of his own heritage.

**Avi**
*Shadrach's Crossing*
Pantheon 1983
Grades 5–8

This story is about smuggling during Prohibition.

**Baker, Betty**
*The Great Desert Race*
Macmillan 1980
Grades 7–9

In 1908 two young women compete in a two-day race using a steam-powered car.

**Beatty, Patricia**
*Eight Mules from Monterey*
Morrow 1982
Grades 7–9

In 1916 a group of people cross the California mountains.

**Bess, Clayton**
*Tracks*
Houghton 1986
Grades 7–9

During the Depression two brothers ride the rails.

**Bolton, Carol**
*Never Jam Today*
Atheneum 1971
Grades 6–9

A young girl works for the suffragettes.

**Branscum, Robbie**
*The Ugliest Boy*
Lothrop 1978
Grades 5–7

A boy grows up in rural Arkansas during the Depression.

**Brink, Carol**
*Ryrie Louly*
Macmillan 1974
Grades 6–8

Left alone for the summer of 1908, a 15-year-old girl has adventures with her siblings and friends in Idaho.

**Bylinsky, Tatyana**
*Before the Wildflowers Bloom*
Crown 1989
Grades 3–5
   An 8-year-old girl grows up in a Colorado mining town in 1916.

**Cahan, Abraham**
*The Rise of David Levinsky*
Harper 1966 [1917]
Grades 9–12
   The novel characterizes life in Czarist Russia, New York's Lower East Side Jewish ghetto, and the garment industry in this story of a successful but lonely man.

**Cather, Willa**
*My Antonia*
Houghton 1973 [1918]
Grades 9–12
   The novel covers thirty years in the life of Antonia, who came to the Nebraska prairie from Bohemia at the turn of the century.

**Cleaver, Vera and Bill**
*Dust of the Earth*
Lippincott 1975
Grades 7–9
   A girl and her family survive the rigors of life in the Dakotas of 1920.

**Conrad, Pam**
*Prairie Song*
Harper 1985
Grades 5–8
   A 12-year-old girl tells about living in a sod house on the Nebraska prairie during the 1900s.

**Constant, Alberta Wilson**
*Does Anyone Care about Lou Emma Miller?*
Crowell 1979
Grades 5–8

The suffragettes try to elect a woman mayor in a pre-World War I Kansas town.

**Crane, Stephen**
*Maggie: A Girl of the Streets* and *George's Mother*
Vintage 1989 [1893, 1896]
Grades 9–12
   These two short novels deal with the New York slums in the early 1900s.

**Cross, Helen Reeder**
*Isabella Mine*
Lothrop 1982
Grades 5–7
   A family lives in a Tennessee mining town in the 1930s.

**de Angeli, Marguerite**
*The Lion in the Box*
Doubleday 1975
Grades 4–6
   A poor family in New York City in the early 1900s has a special Christmas.

**Doctorow, E. L.**
*Ragtime*
Fawcett 1987 [1975]
Grades 10–12
   The lives of three American families become intertwined with the famous and the infamous in the early 1900s.

**Doig, Ivan**
*English Creek*
Penguin 1985
Grades 7–9
   A boy grows up in Montana during the Depression.

**Dos Passos, John**
*Manhattan Transfer*
Houghton 1953
Grades 10–12
   Through Ellen Thatcher the reader gets a

microscopic view of New York City life in the early 1900s.

**Edmonds, Walter**
*Bert Breen's Barn*
Little 1975
Grades 6–8
In 1910 the son and grandson of shiftless folks work toward owning an old but strong barn.

**Edwards, Pat**
*Nelda*
Houghton 1987
Grades 5–9
During the Depression a tight, affectionate family become migrant workers.

**Ellison, Lucille Watkins**
*Butter on Both Sides*
Scribner 1979
Grades 4–6
The story deals with a family in rural Alabama during the early 1900s.

**Fitzgerald, F. Scott**
*The Great Gatsby*
Arion 1984 [1925]
Grades 9–12
Gatsby and Daisy epitomize the sparkling, scintillating, flashy life of the roaring twenties.

**Gaines, Ernest J.**
● *The Autobiography of Miss Jane Pitman*
Doubleday 1971
Grades 9–12
A fictional autobiography of a young woman who is born into slavery, freed after the Civil War, and lives to see the changes during the next one hundred years.

**Geras, Adele**
*Voyage*
Atheneum 1983
Grades 9–12

A group of young Jewish immigrants experience a two-week voyage in steerage.

**Glaser, Dianne**
*The Diary of Trilby Frost*
Holiday 1976
Grades 7–9
An adolescent grows up in the rural United States in the early 1900s.

**Hamlin, Liz**
*I Remember Valentine*
Dutton 1987
Grades 7–9
The Depression is seen through the eyes of an 11-year-old girl.

**Humphreys, Josephine**
*Rich in Love*
Penguin 1988
Grades 7–9
A girl in a South Carolina coastal town adjusts to changes that are caused by unstable economic conditions in her community.

**Hunt, Irene**
*No Promises in the Wind*
Berkley 1987 [1970]
Grades 7–10
The Grandowski boys struggle during the Depression.

**Irwin, Hadley**
● *I Be Somebody*
Signet 1990
Grades 7–9
In 1919, in a small Oklahoma town, an African-American boy tries to understand "Jim Crow" and "Grandfather Clause."

**Kherdian, David**
*A Song for Uncle Harry*
Philomel 1989
Grades 4–6
This is a fictionalized memoir of growing up

Armenian in Wisconsin between two World Wars.

**Lee, Mildred**
*The Rock and the Willow*
Lothrop 1963
Grades 6–8
  The effects of the Depression are seen through the eyes of an Alabama truck farm family.

**Lenski, Lois**
*The Witch of Fourth Street and Other Stories*
Harper 1972
Grades 4–7
  This is a collection of eight stories about the Lithuanian, Irish, Greek, Italian, and Russian immigrants who lived on New York's Lower East Side in the 1920s.

**Lewis, Sinclair**
*Main Street*
New American Library 1961 [1920]
Grades 10–12
  It is clear that change cannot be mandated from the outside and must come from within in this story about life in Gopher Prairie, Minnesota, in the early 1900s.

**Marquand, John P.**
*The Late George Apley*
Modern Library 1948 [1936]
Grades 10–12
  The novel depicts life in upper-class, old Bostonian families and the inevitability of change.

**Mays, Lucinda**
*The Other Shore*
Atheneum 1979
Grades 6–9
  In 1911 a young Italian girl and her family settle in New York where they keep many of the old ways and selectively adopt new ones.

**McNichols, Charles**
■ *Crazy Weather*

Viking 1978
Grades 9–12
  A half-Mojave, half-white boy realizes that he cannot be a Mojave and cannot follow the plans of his white mother.

**Meyerson, Evelyn Wilde**
*The Cat Who Escaped from Steerage*
Scribner 1990
Grades 4–6
  At the turn of the century a Jewish family emigrates from Poland on the steerage deck of a ship.

**Naylor, Phyllis Reynolds**
*Walking through the Dark*
Atheneum 1976
Grades 6–9
  A girl experiences the consequences of poverty during the Depression.

**O'Hara, John**
*Appointment in Samarra*
Random 1982
Grades 9–12
  The novel depicts the effects of the Depression and Prohibition on the upper-middle class.

**Olsen, Violet**
*The Growing Season*
Atheneum 1982
Grades 5–7
  An 11-year-old girl grows up on an Iowa farm during the Depression and acquires skill in learning to surmount her poverty.

**Olsen, Tillie**
*Yonnondio*
Dell 1975
Grades 9–12
  During the Depression a family is brutalized by poverty and they migrate to an industrial center to try to improve their condition.

**Parini, Jay**
*The Patch Boys*
Holt 1986
Grades 9–12

Life in a Pennsylvania mining town in the 1920s is seen through the eyes of a 15-year-old boy.

**Perez, N. A.**
*Breaker*
Houghton 1988
Grades 5–9

A 14-year-old boy goes to work in the coal mines and becomes involved in the 1902 mine workers' strike.

**Potter, Marina**
*A Chance Wild Apple*
Morrow 1982

A girl grows up on a Missouri farm during the Depression.

**Precek, Katherine Wilson**
*Penny in the Road*
Macmillan 1989
Grades 4–5

A 1793 coin, found in 1913, is the basis for this novel that clearly shows changes at home and on the farm.

**Richard, Adrienne**
*Pistol Little*
1990
Grades 7–9

During the Depression a boy comes of age on the range.

**Russo, Richard**
*Mohawk*
Vintage 1989
Grades 11–12

The people in an upstate New York town are tied to the tanneries that are closing down.

**Sebestyen, Ouida**
*Far from Home*
Little 1980
Grades 8–12

In 1929 Texas, after his mother dies, a 13-year-old boy follows instructions left in a note by his mother and goes to a decaying boarding house where he makes a new life.

**Shaw, Margaret**
*A Widder Tomorrow*
Holiday 1990
Grades 9–12

A girl asks her grandmother for advice about following her own or her boyfriend's future. Her grandmother answers by telling her about her life as an ambulance driver in World War I and as a suffragette campaigning for women's rights.

**Sinclair, Upton**
*The Jungle*
Heritage 1965 [1905]
Grades 10–12

A Lithuanian immigrant and his large family come to Chicago in 1900 where he finds work in the stockyards. The novel exposes both the bad working conditions as well as the unsanitary conditions in the meat industry.

**Skurzynski, Gloria**
*The Tempering*
Clarion 1983
Grades 6–9

In 1912 a 15-year-old boy works in a steel mill, loses his job, falls in love, and learns to make compromises.

**Smith, Betty**
*A Tree Grows in Brooklyn*
Harper 1968
Grades 9–12

A girl grows up in the slums of Brooklyn in the early 1900s.

**Snyder, Zilpha Keatley**
*The Velvet Room*
Dell 1988

Grades 4–6

A 12-year-old girl and her family find make-shift homes and try to survive during the Depression.

**Steinbeck, John**
*The Grapes of Wrath*
Penguin 1986 [1939]
Grades 10–12

During the Depression dispossessed Oklahoma landowners migrate from the Dust Bowl to California to find a better life, and fail.

**Steinbeck, John**
*In Dubious Battle*
Penguin 1979 [1936]
Grades 10–12

Jim Nolan organizes migratory workers in California.

**Stoltz, Mary**
*Ivy Larkin*
Dell 1989
Grades 4–6

During the Depression a 14-year-old girl thinks she should not be in an expensive boarding school.

**Tarkington, Booth**
*The Magnificent Ambersons*
Smith 1967 [1918]
Grades 10–12

After the major made a fortune in 1873 the Ambersons of Midland, Indiana, were its leading citizens for two generations. But with the coming of the Industrial Revolution to the region, "old wealth" is pushed aside by "new wealth."

**Taylor, Mildred**
● *The Friendship*
Dial 1987
Grades 3–6

In a rural Mississippi town during the 1930s a black man challenges a white storekeeper to keep a promise.

**Taylor, Mildred**
● *Let the Circle Be Unbroken*
Dial 1981
Grades 6–10

The sequel to *Roll of Thunder, Hear My Cry* continues the chronicle of the Logan family.

**Taylor, Mildred**
● *Roll of Thunder, Hear My Cry*
Bantam 1984
Grades 7–10

The Logan family has to deal with racial brutality, unfairness, and inequity in a small Mississippi town.

**Taylor, Mildred**
● *Song of the Trees*
Dial 1975
Grades 4–6

A rural African-American family in Mississippi during the Depression tries to save the forest on their land.

**Taylor, Sydney**
*[A series of four books about a family]*
*All-of-a-Kind Family*
Dell 1980 [1951]
Grades 4–6

Five Jewish girls grow up on the Lower East Side of New York City in the early 1900s.

_____.
*All-of-A-Kind Family Downtown*
Dell 1989 [1952]
Grades 4–6

This is a continuation of the adventures of the five sisters and their little brother.

_____.
*All-of-A-Kind Family Uptown*
Dell 1989 [1958]
Grades 4–6

The family settles in the Bronx.

_____.
*More All-of-A-Kind Family*
Dell 1989 [1954]
Grades 4–6

The girls and their new baby brother spend their last year in the old neighborhood and the reader shares in the Old World customs in 1914 New York City.

Tolliver, Ruby C.
*Blind Bess, Buddy, and Me*
Hendrick-Long 1990
Grades 4–6

A 10-year-old boy recalls life on his grandfather's Texas farm during the Depression.

Trumbo, Dalton
*Johnny Got His Gun*
Bantam 1984 [1939]
Grades 10–12

The story takes place during World War I and deals with a seriously wounded soldier who is both literally and figuratively a basket case. This is a strong antiwar novel.

Uchida, Yoshiko
*A Jar of Dreams*
Atheneum 1981
Grades 3–5

An 11-year-old girl is the only girl in a Japanese-American family. Set during the Depression, the girl has to cope with financial pressures and increased prejudice because of escalating economic competition.

Uchida, Yoshiko
*The Happiest Ending*
Atheneum 1985
Grades 5–7

In 1936 a 12-year-old Japanese-American girl tries to stop an arranged marriage between a young girl coming over from Japan and a man twice her age.

van Raven, Pieter
*A Time of Troubles*
Scribner 1990
Grades 7–12

During the Depression a boy's father gets out of prison and finds no job opportunities in the Chesapeake Bay area. The two strike out for California where the boy finds a job with the fruit pickers and the father finds a job with the fruit growers.

Villarreal, Jose
*Antonio Pocho*
Anchor 1970
Grades 9–12

During the Depression a Mexican-American boy and his family struggle to survive in California.

Warren, Robert Penn
*All the King's Men*
Harcourt 1983 [1946]
Grades 9–12

The story is a study of the effects of the corruption of power and the price paid to get to the top.

Weingand, Roberta
*The Year of the Comet*
Bradbury 1984
Grades 5–7

A girl grows up in rural Nebraska during the early 1900s.

Weissenberg, Fran
*The Streets Are Paved with Gold*
Harbinger 1990
Grades 7–9

A 14-year-old girl grows up in Brooklyn in the 1920s.

Wharton, Edith
*The House of Mirth* (edited with an introduction by W. B. Lewis)
Houghton 1963 [1905]
Grades 10–12

This book gives a vivid picture of New York society in the Gilded Age—with matchless descriptions of the homes and habits of the idle rich.

**Wood, Jane Roberts**
*The Train to Estelline*
Dell 1988
Grades 9–12
At the turn of the century a young woman teacher joins the pioneers.

**Wright, Richard**
● *Native Son*
Harper 1989 [1940]
Grades 9–12
An African-American man is accused of a crime and must be judged in the white man's world where justice demands death.

**Yep, Laurence**
*Dragonwings*
Harper 1977
Grades 5–9
At the time of the San Francisco earthquake in 1903 a Chinese boy helps his father's dream come true.

**Zeier, Joan T.**
*The Elderberry Thicket*
Atheneum 1990
Grades 4–7
During the Depression a girl's father must leave home to find work and tragedy threatens the family.

## The United States Becomes a World Leader 1940–1990

**Armstrong, William**
● *Sour Land*
Harper 1971
Grades 7–9
An African-American teacher lives his life avoiding conflict and violence but as a result of racism he is senselessly murdered.

**Arnow, Harriette**
*The Dollmaker*
University of Kentucky Press 1985
Grades 10–12
A "hillbilly" family leaves Kentucky for a Detroit housing project so the husband can work in a factory that is producing material for World War II. The family finds its surroundings to be both intimidating and frightening.

**Baker, Betty**
■ *The Shaman's Last Raid*
Harper 1973
Grades 6–9
Eleven-year-old twins share in the fun when their grandfather, an Apache shaman, works with a TV crew.

**Bauer, Marion Dane**
*Rain of Fire*
Clarion 1983
Grades 5–8
A boy is confused by his older brother's behavior when he returns from Hiroshima after World War II.

**Benchley, Nathaniel**
*A Necessary End*
Harper 1976
Grades 9–12
Through diary entries the reader sees a new navy recruit grow to a seasoned veteran in World War II.

**Betancourt, Jeanne**
*More Than Meets the Eye*
Bantam 1990
Grades 7–9
A sophomore in high school takes responsibility for "Americanizing" a Khmer speaking Cambodian girl.

**Borland, Hal**
■ *When the Legends Die*
Bantam 1984 [1963]
Grades 7–12
A Ute Indian boy in Colorado is torn between his own heritage and that of whites.

**Boyd, Candy Dawson**
*Charlie Pippin*
Macmillan 1987
Grades 4–7
Charlie's father is a Vietnam veteran and in order to understand his behavior, Charlie decides that she has to understand that war.

**Bryson, Jamie S.**
■ *The War Canoe*
Alaska Northwest 1990
Grades 9–12
A 17-year-old Tlingit Indian goes through the rites of passage on his small island off the southeast coast of Alaska and finds his heritage.

**Bunting, Eve**
*How Many Days to America?*
Clarion 1988
Grades 4–8
A family emigrates from the Caribbean because of political reasons and enters the U.S. illegally.

**Calvert, Patricia**
■ *The Hour of the Wolf*
Scribner 1983
Grades 7–9
When his friend Danny Yumiat dies, Jake takes his place in the 1,000-mile dogsled race from Anchorage to Nome.

**Cannon, A. E.**
■ *The Shadow Brothers*
Delacorte 1990
Grades 7–10
At age seven, a Navajo boy comes to live with a family in Utah and he and his foster brother, both fifteen, are close and good friends. When a Hopi Indian enrolls in their high school a strain is put on their friendship.

**Caputo, Phillip**
*A Rumor of War*
Ballantine 1987
Grades 10–12
The novel reflects the troubled conscience of America regarding the Vietnam War.

**Carlson, Natalie Savage**
● *The Empty Schoolhouse*
Harper 1965
Grades 3–6
A 10-year-old African-American girl attends a newly desegregated school in Louisiana and experiences both expectations and apprehensions.

**Christian, Mary Blount**
*Dead Man in Catfish Bay*
Whitman 1985
Grades 5–7
Set against economic, political, and social considerations is the story of a Vietnamese girl who enlists the help of a friend to prove her brother innocent of murder.

**Clymer, Eleanor**
■ *The Spider, the Cave and the Pottery Bowl*
Dell 1989 [1971]
Grades 4–6
Two Hopi children, a brother and a sister, spend the summer on the mesa with their grandmother while their father works in town.

**Cole, Norma**
*The Final Tide*
McElderry 1990
Grades 5–8
In 1948 the Wolf Creek Dam in rural Kentucky is completed and a family is uprooted and forced to move.

**Crew, Linda**
*Children of the River*
Delacorte 1989
Grades 7–12

A teenage girl escapes from the Khmer Rouge in Cambodia and comes to Oregon with her aunt's family.

**Curry, Richard**
*Fatal Light*
Penguin 1989
Grades 9–12

This is a fictional account of a marine medic through combat, illness, occupation, and the painful return to the United States.

**Del Vecchio, John**
*The 13th Valley*
Bantam 1984
Grades 11–12

The novel focuses on twelve days in the life of an airborne infantry company in Vietnam.

**Dexter, Peter**
*Paris Trout*
Penguin 1989
Grades 11–12

A small Georgia town is shattered by racial murder and sexual violence.

**Distad, Audree**
■ *Dakota Sons*
Harper 1972
Grades 3–6

A white boy makes friends with a Dakota Sioux and in spite of the prejudice that surrounds them, their friendship remains intact.

**Dorris, Michael**
■ *A Yellow Raft in Blue Water*
Holt 1987
Grades 9–12

Three generations of Native American women, each from her own perspective, help Rayona in her tortured search for self-identity.

**Edwards, Pat**
● *Little John and Plutie*
Houghton 1988
Grades 4–7

A 9-year-old boy learns about the effects of segregation from his African-American friends.

**Ellison, Ralph**
● *Invisible Man*
Random 1972 [1952]
Grades 10–12

An African-American man who travels north has to deal with others' preconceived ideas about him.

**Faulkner, William**
● *Intruder in the Dust*
Random 1972 [1948]
Grades 10–12

A young white boy in Mississippi tries to save an elderly African-American man who is accused of murder.

**Fife, Dale**
■ *Ride the Crooked Wind*
Coward, McCann 1973
Grades 5–7

After the death of his parents a Paiute Indian boy goes to live with his grandmother. When she is hospitalized he is sent to the Indian Boarding School where he must learn new ways.

**Forkner, Ben and Patrick (eds.)**
● *Stories of the Modern South*
Penguin 1986
Grades 7–12

William Faulkner, Tennessee Williams, Eudora Welty, and other writers portray the many faces of the modern South.

**Gaines, Ernest**
● *A Gathering of Old Men*
Knopf 1983
Grades 9–12

A number of old African-American men and one

white woman confess to the killing of a white man in Louisiana. Each has a good motive.

**George, Jean Craighead**
■ *Julie of the Wolves*
Harper 1987 [1972]
Grades 7–9

A 13-year-old Eskimo girl who is lost on the tundra is protected by a wolf pack and in the process comes to appreciate her heritage.

**George, Jean Craighead**
■ *The Talking Earth*
Harper 1983
Grades 6–9

Because she questioned the beliefs of her tribe a Seminole Indian girl is disciplined and sent alone into the Florida Everglades.

**George, Jean Craighead**
■ *Water Sky*
Harper 1987
Grades 7–9

In modern-day Barrow, Alaska, a young New England boy, under the guidance of an Eskimo captain, discovers what life is like in an Alaskan whaling camp.

**Girion, Barbara**
■ *Indian Summer*
Scholastic 1990
Grades 6–9

A middle-class white American girl and an Iroquois Indian girl are forced to spend a summer together on an Iroquois reservation. In order to survive the summer the girls must come to grips with the misunderstandings and intolerance that result from differences in their cultures.

**Glasser, Ronald J.**
*Another War, Another Peace*
Ballantine 1986
Grades 10–12

A doctor and the soldier assigned to protect him confront the realities of the Vietnam War.

**Green, Connie Jordan**
*The War at Home*
McElderry 1989
Grades 6–8

A family suffers as a result of the manufacture of an atom bomb at the Oak Ridge, Tennessee, plant.

**Greene, Bette**
*Summer of My German Soldier*
Bantam 1984 [1973]
Grades 6–10

In an Arkansas town during World War II a 12-year-old Jewish girl becomes friends with a German prisoner of war.

**Greenfield, Eloise**
● *Sister*
Harper 1987 [1974]
Grades 6–8

A 13-year-old African-American girl rereads her five-year diary and comes to understand who she is.

**Griese, Arnold A.**
● *The Wind Is Not a River*
Crowell 1978
Grades 4–7

This realistic treatment of war involves two Aleut children who find an injured Japanese soldier during the invasion of their island.

**Grove, Vicki**
*Goodbye My Wishing Star*
Putnam 1988
Grades 4–6

A girl's family is losing their farm and she records her life during the last twelve weeks of their stay and leaves the diary in the barn for the new family.

**Hale, Janet C.**
■ *The Owl's Song*
Avon 1976
Grades 7–10

An Indian boy leaves his Idaho reservation and goes to California where he faces bigotry and isolation.

**Hamilton, Virginia**
● *The House of Dies Drear*
Macmillan 1968
Grades 5–9

A mystery story about an African-American family in Ohio who move into the former home of an abolitionist who used the house as a stop on the underground railroad.

**Harris, Marilyn**
■ *Hatter-Fox*
Random 1973
Grades 9–12

A 17-year-old Navajo girl with a criminal record becomes friends with a white woman doctor who helps her survive a cruel and indifferent bureaucracy.

**Herlihy, Dirlie**
● *Ludie's Song*
Puffin 1990
Grades 5–9

A girl from the North visits a family in Macon, Georgia, and befriends an African-American woman who is scarred and cannot speak but who is bright, worthy, and artistic.

**Hill, Kirkpatrick**
■ *Toughboy and Sister*
McElderry 1990
Grades 4–7

When the parents of two Athabascan Indian children die the children learn to survive in the Alaskan wilderness.

**Holling, Holling C.**
■ *Paddle to the Sea*
Houghton 1989
Grades 9–12

An Indian boy travels through the Great Lakes in a small canoe and reaches the Atlantic Ocean.

**Holman, Felice**
*Secret City, U.S.A.*
Scribner 1990
Grades 5–9

Benno and his friends try to extricate themselves from their life in the barrio.

**Houston, James**
■ *River Runners: A Tale of Hardship and Bravery*
Atheneum 1979
Grades 7–9

A 15-year-old boy comes to work at an Alaskan trading post in Naskapi Territory and with the help of a Naskapi boy learns skills that allow him to survive the journey to a trading post in winter.

**Houston, James**
■ *Spirit Wrestler*
Harcourt 1980
Grades 7–9

This is the story of an Inuit shaman on Baffin Island in the 1950s.

**Irwin, Hadley**
*Kim/Kimi*
McElderry 1987
Grades 7–9

A 16-year-old half-Japanese-American girl's experiences during World War II cause her to search for her identity and accept the best of both heritages.

**Jones, James**
*From Here to Eternity*
Dell 1985 [1951]
Grades 10–12

This novel provides a graphic picture of army life in World War II.

**Kadohata, Cynthia**
*The Floating World*
Viking 1989
Grades 9–12

In the northwest of the 1950s, a 12-year-old

Japanese girl grows up amid prejudice.

**Krumhold, Joseph**
*And Now Miguel*
Harper 1989 [1953]
Grades 6–8
 A Hispanic boy has problems growing up in New Mexico.

**Lafarge, Oliver**
■ *Laughing Boy*
Signet 1971 [1929]
Grades 10–12
 Two young Navajos, a boy and a girl, try to preserve their heritage but face many conflicts because, surprisingly, the Indians are a significant percentage of the population.

**Lampman, Evelyn**
*Go up the Road*
Atheneum 1972
Grades 5–8
 A 12-year-old Mexican American and her family of migrant workers see the possibility of a more stable life.

**Lee, Harper**
● *To Kill a Mockingbird*
Warner 1982 [1960]
Grades 9–12
 A lawyer defends an African-American man accused of raping a white woman in a small Alabama town.

**Lesley, Craig**
■ *Winterkill*
Dell 1986
Grades 10–12
 A northwest American Indian tries to teach his defiant son about the traditions of his people before they are lost forever.

**Levitan, Sonia**
*Silver Days*
Atheneum 1989

Grades 7–9
 A Jewish family escapes from Nazi Germany and has to make a new life in the United States.

**Levoy, Myron**
*Alan and Naomi*
Harper 1977
Grades 6–9
 A refugee girl from Nazi-occupied Paris and an American boy live in the same apartment house and become friends. He tries to help her recover from the effects of the Holocaust.

**Lo, Stephen C.**
*The Incorporation of Eric Chung*
Algonquin 1989
Grades 9–12
 This is a droll tale about a boy's emigration from China to Texas to attend college. He stays in the United States and joins a company wanting to do business with China only to find his admiration for the business world wanes as he experiences its negatives.

**Locker, Thomas**
*Family Farm*
Dial 1988
Grades 2–6
 A family faces the trauma of losing their farm for which they have worked hard and about which they cared deeply.

**MacKinnon, Bernie**
● *The Mealtime*
Houghton 1984
Grades 9–12
 An African-American family lives in a white suburb and has to face the enmity and animosity of neighbors.

**Mason, Bobbie Ann**
*In Country*
Harper 1985
Grades 9–12
 A girl struggles to understand the Vietnam

War, a war in which her father died and a war that damaged her uncle psychologically.

**Mazer, Norma Fox**
*Downtown*
Morrow 1984
Grades 7–12

Pete's parents are antiwar activists who are hiding from the authorities and he has come to grips with his desire for an ordinary life and his parents' beliefs and behavior.

**Mazer, Harry**
*The Last Mission*
Dell 1981
Grades 6–10

A 15-year-old boy uses his brother's birth certificate, enlists in the U.S. Air Force, becomes a gunner on a B-17, and ends up as a German prisoner of war.

**McMillan, Terry (ed.)**
● *Breaking Ice: An Anthology of
Contemporary American Black Fiction*
Penguin 1990
Grades 9–12

More than seventy-five authors portray the African-American experience through their stories.

**Messer, Ronald K.**
● *Shumway*
Nelson 1975
Grades 6–8

In the 1950s South, two poor boys, one white and one African American, have an uneasy friendship.

**Mohr, Nicholasa**
*El Bronx Remembered: A Novella and Stories*
Harper 1975
Grades 7–9

Twelve stories deal with the suffering and beauty of the inner city Spanish-American community.

**Mohr, Nicholasa**
*Felita*
Dial 1979
Grades 3–6

When a girl and her family move away from the barrio they meet so much hostility because of prejudice and bigotry that they return to the barrio.

**Mohr, Nicholasa**
*Going Home*
Bantam 1989
Grades 4–6

A 12-year-old girl discovers her heritage during a summer visit to Puerto Rico.

**Mohr, Nicholasa**
*Nilda*
Harper 1973
Grades 7–9

In the early 1940s a girl grows up in Spanish Harlem.

**Morrison, Toni**
● *Sula*
Plume 1987 [1973]
Grades 9–12

This is a re-creation of the African-American experience in the United States over a forty-year period.

**Morrison, Toni**
● *Tar Baby*
Plume 1987 [1981]
Grades 9–12

This is a love story that portrays the quandary of African-American identity.

**Myers, Walter Dean**
● *Fallen Angels*
Scholastic 1989
Grades 9–12

An African-American boy who thought he grew up tough in Harlem found out what toughness really was during his tour of Vietnam with all its bloodiness, ferocity, inhumanity, and savageness.

**Naylor, Gloria**
● *The Women of Brewster Place*
Penguin 1988
Grades 9–12
Seven interwoven stories depict the lives of African-American women today.

**Nelson, Theresa**
*And One for All*
Orchard 1989
Grades 6–9
The controversy surrounding the Vietnam War becomes clear in this story about a loving family and their friends.

**Neufeld, John**
● *Edgar Allan*
Signet 1990 [1968]
Grades 5–9
A white family adopts an African-American child and suffers severe repercussions.

**Nicol, C. W.**
■ *The White Shaman*
Little 1979
Grades 7–9
A boy is adopted by Eskimos and learns to live and think as they do.

**O'Brien, Tim**
*Going After Cacciato*
Doubleday 1989 [1978]
Grades 11–12
A soldier walks away from the Vietnam War and his friends explore their lives in searching for him.

**O'Dell, Scott**
■ *Black Star, Bright Star*
Fawcett 1990
Grades 7–9
A girl takes her father's place in the Iditarod, the grueling dogsled race in Alaska.

**Paterson, Katherine**
*Park's Quest*
Penguin 1989
Grades 5–8
This is a look at the Vietnam War from the viewpoint of the children of veterans whose lives have been affected by a war that seems obscure and ill defined.

**Paulsen, Gary**
*The Crossing*
Orchard 1987
Grades 6–8
A 13-year-old street child is helped by an American soldier to cross the Mexican border.

**Paulsen, Gary**
■ *Dogsong*
Bradbury 1985
Grades 9–12
An Eskimo boy learns about his heritage when he makes a 1,400 mile trip with a sled and dog team.

**Paulsen, Gary**
*The Winter Room*
Orchard 1989
Grades 6–8
An old Norwegian uncle explains to his nephew what life was like on a Minnesota farm.

**Porte, Barbara Ann**
● *I Only Made up the Roses*
Greenwillow 1987
Grades 5–8
This is the story of three generations of an interracial family.

**Potoki, Chaim**
*The Chosen*
Fawcett 1986 [1967]
Grades 9–12
Life in an Hasidic/Orthodox Jewish community

in Brooklyn leads two boys from different Jewish cultures to become friends.

*Davita's Harp*
Fawcett 1986
Grades 10–12
    In New York City in the 1930s and 1940s a young girl embraces the faith her mother abandoned.

*In the Beginning*
Fawcett 1986 [1975]
Grades 10–12
    This is a portrayal of Jewish life in the United States from the 1920s through the 1940s.

*My Name is Asher Lev*
Fawcett 1984 [1972]
Grades 10–12
    A contemporary artist becomes alienated from the world into which he was born.

Poynter, Margaret
*A Time Too Swift*
Atheneum 1990
Grades 5–7
    A girl who lives in San Diego is caught up in the events following the attack on Pearl Harbor and is profoundly affected.

Pryor, Bonnie
*The House on Maple Street*
Morrow 1987
Grades 3–6
    A family moves into a house on Maple Street and the author takes the reader back three hundred years to see all the people and events that preceded the move.

Reibel, Paula
*A Morning Moon*
Berkley 1986

Grades 7–9
    A Hungarian family emigrates to the United States and must make many hard-to-understand and tough adjustments to life in this country.

Rivera, Edward
*Family Installments*
Penguin 1983
Grades 9–12
    This is a vivid account of a family's migration from rural Puerto Rico to New York City and what it means to grow up Hispanic.

Rogers, Jean
■ *Goodbye, My Island*
Greenwillow 1983
Grades 5–7
    A 12-year-old Eskimo girl tells about her life since the 1964 government decision that closed her school on King Island in the Bering Sea.

Rosen, Kenneth (ed.)
■ *The Man to Send Rain Clouds*
Vintage 1975
Grades 9–12
    Nineteen short stories illustrate the conflict between Indian heritage and status in today's society.

Rostkowski, Margaret
*After the Dancing Days*
Harper 1989
Grades 7–9
    Two high school students are at odds with their father regarding the Vietnam War.

Savage, Cindy
*Project: Makeover*
Horizon 1990
Grades 6–9
    A group of girls welcome new Vietnamese teenagers to their school and in the process of "Americanizing" them create many problems.

Shange, Ntozake
● *Betsy Brown*
St. Martin's 1986
Grades 9–12

This book is a family portrait of three generations of African-American women in 1957 St. Louis, the year of its school desegregation.

Shotwell, Louise
*Magdalena*
Dell 1989
Grades 7–10

A Puerto Rican girl in a U. S. city helps her grandmother accept the new with the old.

Silko, Leslie Marmon
■ *Ceremony*
Penguin 1986 [1977]
Grades 7–9

After World War II, an Indian returns to his tribe and confronts the conflicts between modern life and tribal traditions.

Singer, Marilyn
*Several Kinds of Silence*
Harper 1988
Grades 7–9

A girl has a Japanese boyfriend but is fearful of telling this to her father who blames the Japanese for his unemployment.

Sneve, Virginia Driving Hawk
■ *High Elk's Treasure*
Holiday 1972
Grades 4–6

This is a fictionalized account of a Lakota Sioux family today.

Sneve, Virginia Driving Hawk
■ *Jimmy Yellow Hawk*
Holiday 1972
Grades 7–9

A modern Sioux Indian lives on a reservation in South Dakota and combines old and new ways.

Sneve, Virginia Driving Hawk
■ *When Thunders Spoke*
Holiday 1974
Grades 7–9

A boy lives with his parents on the Dakota Reservation and conflict arises between them regarding how Native Americans should live in today's world.

Sone, Monica Itoi
*Nisei Daughter*
University of Washington Press 1979
Grades 7–10

A Japanese-American family is interned during World War II.

Sorenson, Virginia
*Plain Girl*
Harcourt 1989
Grades 9–12

An Amish girl finds out that she can remain true to her principles and still accept new ways.

Southall, Ivan
*The Long Night Watch*
Farrar 1984
Grades 9–12

A soldier during World War II causes the death of most of the religious refugees on a solitary island in the South Pacific.

Springer, Nancy
● *They're All Named Wildfire*
Atheneum 1989
Grades 5–7

A friendship between an African-American girl and a white girl survives bigotry.

Storm, Hyemeyohsts
■ *Song of Heyoehkah*
Ballantine 1983
Grades 10–12

This is the story of a Plains Indian couple who try to maintain their cultural heritage in a white society.

**Tamar, Erika**
*Good-bye Glamour Girl*
Lippincott 1984
Grades 5–7

Liesl is eager to become a real American when her family escapes from Nazi Austria during World War II.

**Tate, Eleanor**
● *The Secret of Gumbo Grove*
Bantam 1988
Grades 5–8

An 11-year-old South Carolina girl traces her community's history through stories about people in the local graveyard.

**Taylor, Mildred**
● *The Gold Cadillac*
Dial 1987
Grades 3–5

In the 1950s when an African-American family drives to the South in their new car, a girl comes face to face with prejudice and fear.

**Taylor, Mildred**
● *The Road to Memphis*
Dial 1990
Grades 7–10

This story of the Logan family takes place in Mississippi in 1941 and deals with the unfair justice system, white oppression, and prejudice.

**Thomas, Joyce C.**
● *Bright Shadow*
Avon 1983
Grades 6–9

This is an African-American woman's story about how peace was destroyed in her rural Oklahoma hometown. It is a story of love, loss, and self-discovery.

**Thomas, Piri**
*Down These Mean Streets*
Knopf 1978 [1967]
Grades 7–12

Chronicles the experiences of a young boy growing up in the barrio. (A 1979 court case ordered this book removed from all junior high school libraries in a particular school district.)

**Turner, Ann**
■ *A Hunter Comes Home*
Crown 1980
Grades 9–12

A teenager learns old Inuit ways.

**Uchida, Yoshiko**
*The Best Bad Thing*
Atheneum 1983
Grades 5–7

A Japanese-American girl has to spend the last month of her summer vacation helping out in the house of a widow.

**Uchida, Yoshiko**
*Journey Home*
Aladdin 1982
Grades 6–8

After being released from a concentration camp in Utah, a family returns to California and tries to pick up the pieces of their lives only to meet with discrimination.

**Uchida, Yoshiko**
*Journey to Topaz*
Creative Arts 1985 [1971]
Grades 6–8

After the attack on Pearl Harbor, Japanese Americans living on the west coast are sent to a concentration camp and life changes drastically for a girl and her family.

**Uchida, Yoshiko**
*Picture Bride*
Fireside 1988
Grades 7–9

An arranged marriage brings a young Japanese girl to the United States.

**Van Raven, Pieter**
● *Pickle and Price*
Scribner 1990
Grades 7–10

In the 1950s an African-American man and a white Southern boy travel together across the country and in the process come to understand racial tensions.

**Wallin, Luke**
■ *Ceremony of the Panther*
Bradbury 1987
Grades 6–9

A Florida Indian boy is torn between tradition and modern ways.

**Walter, Mildred Pitts**
● *Have a Happy*
Lothrop 1989
Grades 4–6

The reader comes to know the essence and message of Kwanza, which is a commemoration of the African-American legacy.

**Wartski, Maurice Crane**
*A Long Way from Home*
Westminster 1980
Grades 5–8

A Vietnamese teenager has difficulty adjusting to life in the United States.

**Welch, James**
● *Winter in the Blood*
Penguin 1986 [1974]
Grades 7–9

A Blackfoot Indian tries to reconcile his heritage with the realities of modern reservation life.

**Wharton, William**
*A Midnight Clear*
Ballantine 1984
Grades 9–12

In World War II a group of young U.S. soldiers learn about themselves and "the enemy."

**Whelan, Gloria**
*Silver*
Random 1988
Grades 3–5

This is the story of a 9-year-old daughter of a dogsled racer in Alaska.

**White, Ruth**
*Sweet Creek Holler*
Farrar 1988
Grades 6–12

Based on her own childhood, the author tells about life in a small Appalachian mountain community.

**Wilkinson, Brenda**
● *Ludell*
Harper 1975
Grades 7–9

The story covers three years in the life of an African-American girl in rural Georgia in the mid-1950s.

**Wilkinson, Brenda**
● *Not Separate, Not Equal*
Harper 1987
Grades 3–7

In 1965 an African-American girl finds herself to be one of six students at a newly integrated high school in Georgia.

**Williams, Vera B. and Jennifer**
*Stringbean's Trip to the Shining Sea*
Greenwillow 1988
Grades 3–8

Two brothers travel in a truck from Kansas to the Pacific Ocean and send their grandfather a postcard every day. The grandfather puts the cards, which are full of detail and description, into a scrapbook.

**Yep, Laurence**
*Child of the Owl*
Harper 1977
Grades 7–9

During the 1960s a 12-year-old girl grows up in San Francisco's Chinatown.

**Yep, Laurence**
*Sea Glass*
Harper 1979
Grades 7–9

When a boy moves from San Francisco's Chinatown to small-town Concepcion, he finds himself rejected by two cultures—Chinese and American.

---

**Note:** For good readers who enjoy reading, the following books by James A. Michener are recommended. They have separate annotations because the stories span many centuries and do not fit within the selected time periods below.

**Michener, James A.**
*Alaska*
Fawcett 1989
Grades 10–12

This is a fictionalized account of the history of Alaska from prehistoric times to the present.

_____.
*Centennial*
Fawcett 1989 [1974]
Grades 10–12

This is a fictionalized account of the United States from prehistoric times to the present told through different voices.

_____.
*Chesapeake*
Fawcett 1989 [1978]
Grades 10–12

The story of how the Chesapeake Bay and its surrounding areas have sustained life over the millennia.

_____.
*Hawaii*
Fawcett 1989 [1959]
Grades 10–12

A fictionalized history of the islands from prehistory to the present in the voices of families who were integral it its development.

# WORLD HISTORY

## Prehistoric Times

**Auel, Jean**
*Clan of the Cave Bear*
[Crimean Peninsula]
Bantam 1984
Grades 10–12
   A Cro-Magnon girl-child is adopted into a Neanderthal tribe.

_____.
*The Valley of the Horses*
[Crimean Peninsula]
Bantam 1984
Grades 10–12
   Ayla's story continues after she is expelled by her adopted clan and searches for her own group.

_____.
*The Mammoth Hunters*
[Crimean Peninsula]
Bantam 1986
Grades 10–12
   Ayla joins the mammoth hunters.

**Behn, Harry**
*The Faraway Lurs*
[Denmark]
Hall 1981
Grades 6–9
   A tragic love story that takes place during the Bronze Age.

**Bosse, Malcolm J.**
*Cave beyond Time*
[Arizona]
Crowell 1980
Grades 7–9
   At an archaeological dig, Ben explores three different eras of ancient times.

**Christopher, John**
*Dom and Va*
[Africa]
Macmillan 1973
Grades 6–8
   Five thousand years ago hunters and farmers struggled against each other.

**Denzel, Justin**
*Boy of the Painted Cave*
[?]
Philomel 1988
Grades 5–7
   A crippled boy tries to live independently and paints magic pictures on the wall of his cave.

**Garcia, Ann O'Neal**
*Spirit on the Wall*
[?]
Holiday 1982
Grades 7–10
   Three extremely independent cave people defy their clan.

**Linevski, A. (Trans. by Maria Polushkin)**
*An Old Tale Carved out of Stone*
[Siberia]
Crown 1973
Grades 9–12
   In spite of many trials, a young, insecure shaman tries to lead his tribe wisely.

**McGowen, Tom**
*The Time of the Forest*
[Denmark]
Houghton 1988
Grades 4–7
   A boy and a girl from antagonistic tribes start a new life together.

**Millstead, Thomas**
*Cave of the Morning Shadows*
[?]
Dial 1979
Grades 6–8

A boy grows up in prehistoric times.

**Osborne, Chester**
*The Memory String*
[Siberia to Alaska]
Atheneum 1984
Grades 5–8
   Thirty thousand years ago Indians move from Siberia to Alaska.

**Shuler, Linda Lay**
*She Who Remembers*
[Mesa Verde and Chaco Canyon]
Signet 1989
Grades 7–9
   This story of love and adventure is set in America's prehistoric cities.

**Steele, William O.**
*The Magic Amulet*
[?]
Harcourt 1979
Grades 4–6
   A boy is abandoned by his clan because his lame leg slows them down when they hunt and gather. He is accepted by another clan after leading them to food because of what they perceive to be the powers of his amulet.

**Treece, Henry**
*The Dream-Time*
[United Kingdom (England)]
Meredith 1968
Grades 5–7
   In 11,000 B.C. a lame boy finds that his artistic gifts ostracize him and he travels from tribe to tribe with a friend and an orphan boy.

**Turnbull, Ann**
*Maroo of the Winter Caves*
[?]
Clarion 1984
Grades 3–6
   After her father dies, a girl of the Ice Age leads her family to the tribe's winter camp.

**Turner, Ann**
*Time of the Bison*
[?]
Macmillan 1987
Grades 3–6
   At the time of the cave dwellers a boy gains the respect and admiration of his clan by sculpting lovely clay animals.

## B.C.—A.D. 650

**Bauman, Hans**
*I Marched with Hannibal*
[France and Roman Empire]
Walck 1962
Grades 6–9
   Hannibal's favorite elephant and driver find an orphan boy and take him along with them across the Alps to Rome.

**Beatty, John and Patricia**
*A Donkey for the King*
[Jerusalem]
Macmillan 1966
Grades 6–8
   A mute, homeless young shepherd in the Holy Land who can communicate only with a flute joins a traveling circus and is put in charge of a performing donkey.

**Bradshaw, Gillian**
*The Beacon of Alexandria*
[Egypt]
Houghton 1987
Grades 7–9
   In 293, Charis, who wants to escape an arranged marriage, runs away from Ephesus to Alexandria and plans to study medicine.

**Carter, Dorothy Sharp**
*His Majesty, Queen Hatshepsut*
[Egypt]
Lippincott 1987

Grades 5–10

This is the incredible and extraordinary story of a commanding woman who became the only female Pharaoh of Egypt.

**Dickinson, Peter**
*The Dancing Bear*
[Constantinople (Istanbul)]
Little 1973
Grades 6–9

A slave and his trained bear manage to remain alive during the destruction of Byzantium in 558.

**Haugaard, Erik**
*The Rider and His Horse*
[Jerusalem]
Houghton 1968
Grades 8–10

A boy who is a survivor of the Masada tells the story of the fall of ancient Jerusalem.

**Hunter, Mollie**
*The Stronghold*
[United Kingdom (England)]
Harper 1974
Grades 6–10

To fend off the Romans a crippled boy convinces the Druids to build a fortress of his design along the Scottish coast.

**McGraw, Eloise**
*The Golden Goblet*
[Egypt]
Puffin 1986 [1961]
Grades 6–8

A boy struggles to reveal a terrible crime and reshape his own future.

**McGraw, Eloise**
*Mara, Daughter of the Nile*
[Egypt]
Coward 1953
Grades 6–8

A slave girl spies for the female Pharaoh Hatshepsut and also for Lord Sheftu who works

for the king.

**Morrison, Lucille**
*The Lost Queen of Egypt*
[Egypt]
Lippincott 1937
Grades 7–9

The story of Ankhsenpaaten, daughter of Nefertiti and wife of Tutankhaten, who disappears after the death of her husband.

**Paton Walsh, Jill**
*Crossing to Salamis*
[Greece]
Heinemann 1977
Grades 7–9

Aster leaves Athens in 497 B.C. with her mother, servant, and friend because the Persians invade.

**Paton Walsh, Jill**
*Hengest's Tale*
[Germany]
St. Martin's 1966
Grades 8–10

Hengest remembers what happened when he divided his loyalties between the Jutes, Danes, and Frisians and how it resulted in his death.

**Paton Walsh, Jill**
*Persian Gold*
[Greece]
Heinemann 1978
Grades 7–9

Both Spartans and Athenians have been looking for Themistokles, the Athenian general, whom they believe did not do his best to defeat the Persians.

**Paton Walsh, Jill**
*The Walls of Athens*
[Greece]
Heinemann 1977
Grades 5–7

After the Persian War the walls of Athens must be rebuilt. When a runner falls, the message that the walls are finished is carried to Sparta by a young boy.

**Ray, Mary**
*The Windows of Elissa*
[Carthage (North Africa, Tunisia)]
Faber 1982
Grades 6–8

The story takes place in the third century when the city of Carthage was besieged and Elissa's younger sister is in danger of being sacrificed to Baal in order to save the city.

**Renault, Mary**
*Fire from Heaven*
[Greece]
Vintage 1977 [1969]
Grades 10–12

This is a fictionalized account of Alexander the Great from childhood to the age of twenty when he succeeded his father who was murdered.

**Renault, Mary**
*The Last of the Wine*
[Greece]
Vintage 1975 [1956]
Grades 10–12

The story takes place at the time of Socrates and the world of that time is brought to life.

**Renault, Mary**
*The Mask of Apollo*
[Greece]
Vintage 1988 [1966]
Grades 10–12

An actor in the fourth century B.C. always carries with him the mask of Apollo, the symbol of the god who controls his destiny. This is a good picture of Plato's times.

**Renault, Mary**
*The Praise Singer*
[Greece]
Vintage 1988 [1978]
Grades 10–12

A boy follows a sign from Apollo and ends up in Athens. There he meets the statesmen and artists of the Golden Age of Greece.

**Schlein, Miriam**
*I Tut: The Boy Who Became Pharaoh*
[Egypt]
Four Winds 1978
Grades 3–5

Tut tells the story of his life and, after his death, the story is continued by his friend.

**Seavy, Marquita and Susan**
*The Kindling of the Flame*
[France]
Watts 1988 [1980]
Grades 10–12

This is a story of two brothers of the Arverni tribe of Gaul. One becomes a king, Vercingetorix, and the other a Druid.

**Seredy, Kate**
*The White Stag*
[Hungary]
Viking 1937
Grades 7–9

This is a story about Hungary and about its many leaders including Attila the Hun.

**Speare, Elizabeth George**
*The Bronze Bow*
[Israel]
Houghton 1961
Grades 7–10

A boy is looking to find the real savior among the many who make this claim.

**Stolz, Mary Zemet**
*The Stone Carver*
[Egypt]
Harcourt 1988
Grades 4–6

This is a tale about the origin of the Sphinx that includes the telling of the story in hieroglyphics.

Sutcliff, Rosemary
*The Eagle of the Ninth*
[United Kingdom (England)]
Walck 1954
Grades 9–12
A centurion tries to recapture the eagle standard of the lost Ninth Legion that disappeared while his father was in charge of the army in northern Britain.

Sutcliff, Rosemary
*Frontier Wolf*
[United Kingdom (England)]
Dutton 1980
Grades 10–12
A Roman army officer is punished and sent to lead a motley group in northern England.

Sutcliff, Rosemary
*The Mark of the Horse Lord*
[United Kingdom (England)]
Dell 1989 [1965]
Grades 8–10
When Rome occupied Britain an ex-gladiator is asked to impersonate a prince and regain the throne that was stolen by a wicked queen.

Sutcliff, Rosemary
*Outcast*
[United Kingdom (England)]
Oxford 1955
Grades 9–12
An infant son of a Roman soldier is raised by British foster parents until he is fifteen and then the tribe expels him.

Sutcliff, Rosemary
*The Silver Branch*
[United Kingdom (England)]
Oxford 1958
Grades 9–12
A Roman army surgeon in Britain uncovers a plot to overthrow Emperor Carausius and becomes entangled with an underground group of Roman secret agents.

Sutcliff, Rosemary
*Song for a Dark Queen*
[United Kingdom (England)]
Harper 1979
Grades 7–9
This is a fictionalized account of Queen Boadicea who led the early British tribes in an unsuccessful fight against the Romans.

Sutcliff, Rosemary
*Sun Horse, Moon Horse*
[United Kingdom (England)]
Dutton 1978
Grades 6–9
A boy in pre-Roman England becomes head of his tribe.

Sutcliff, Rosemary
*Warrior Scarlet*
[United Kingdom (England)]
Oxford 1958
Grades 5–7
In 900 B.C. a boy with one good arm practices to be a warrior and to kill a wolf singlehandedly. When he fails he is sent to live with the outcasts but is redeemed when he saves the life of a fellow outcast by killing three wolves.

Trease, Geoffrey
*Message to Hadrian*
[United Kingdom (England)]
Vanguard 1955
Grades 7–9
A boy travels from Britain to Rome carrying a message that will save his friend's life.

Trease, Geoffrey
*Web of Traitors*
[Greece]
Vanguard 1952
Grades 4–7
The story centers on the Athenian plot to overthrow the democracy after the death of Pericles around 425 B.C.

**Treece, Henry**
*The Queen's Brooch*
[United Kingdom (England)]
Putnam 1967
Grades 9–12

A Roman boy grows up with the Celts in Britain and eventually is expected to fight them.

**Treece, Henry**
*War Dog*
[United Kingdom (England)]
Criterion 1963
Grades 7–10

A dog sees and interprets historical events during the era of the Roman Empire.

**Winterfield, Henry**
*Detectives in Togas*
[Italy (Rome)]
Harcourt 1956
Grades 5–7

Some schoolboys are wrongly accused of defacing a temple in ancient Rome.

**Yarbro, Chelsea**
*Locadio's Apprentice*
[Italy]
Harper 1984
Grades 6–9

This is an exciting story that takes place at the time of the eruption of Mt. Vesuvius and the devastation of Pompeii.

## 651–1066

**Almedingen, E. M.**
*A Candle at Dusk*
[France]
Farrar 1969
Grades 6–8

An eighth-century Frankish boy gets his father's permission to live in a neighboring abbey so that he can learn to read.

**Clarke, Pauline**
*Torlor the Fatherless*
[United Kingdom (England)]
Farber 1978
Grades 6–8

A Viking boy is stranded when his ship leaves without him and he is adopted by an earl who dies fighting the Vikings at the Battle of Maldon.

**Clements, Bruce**
*Prison Widow, Jerusalem Blue*
[Scandinavia]
Farrar 1977
Grades 6–8

In 831 an English brother and sister are captured in a raid and become Viking slaves.

**Crossley-Holland, Kevin**
*The Fire-Brother*
[United Kingdom (England)]
Seabury 1975
Grades 6–9

An East Saxon boy converts to Christianity and tries to cope with the hostility of his brother and the villagers toward the monks with whom he lives.

**Crossley-Holland, Kevin**
*Havelock the Dane*
[Denmark and England]
Dutton 1965
Grades 6–9

Based on the legend this is the love story of Havelock and Princess Goldborough of England, both of whom have been deprived of their thrones and intend to regain them.

**Crossley-Holland, Kevin**
*The Sea Stranger*
[United Kingdom (England)]
Seabury 1973
Grades 6–9

A Saxon boy who has never met a Christian wants to be like the compassionate stranger who lands a small boat near his Essex coast home.

**de Angeli, Marguerite**
*Black Fox of Lorne*
[Scandinavia to United Kingdom (Scotland)]
Doubleday 1956
Grades 5–7

During the tenth century twin Norse brothers are shipwrecked off the Scottish coast.

**Haugaard, Erik**
*Hakon of Rogen's Saga*
[Scandinavia]
Houghton 1963
Grades 6–8

A boy is denied his right to Rogen Island by his villainous uncle.

**Haugaard, Erik**
*A Slave's Tale*
[Scandinavia to France]
Houghton 1965
Grades 8–10

A slave girl stows away on a Viking ship when Hakon sails for Brittany.

**Hodges, Walter**
*The Marsh King*
[United Kingdom (England)]
Coward, McCann·1967
Grades 8–10

King Alfred of Wessex tries to keep peace and civilization intact when the Danes invade.

**Hodges, Walter**
*The Namesake*
[United Kingdom (England)]
Coward, McCann 1964
Grades 6–8

An old man remembers his childhood as a crippled scribe in the court of King Alfred the Great.

**Pyle, Howard**
*Otto of the Silver Hand*
[Germany]
Watts 1971 [1888]
Grades 6–9

The son of a robber baron is kidnapped in medieval times.

**Stolz, Mary**
*Pangur Ban*
[Ireland?]
Harper 1988
Grades 7–9

A boy wants to spend his life in a monastery and his father agrees. When the Vikings invade he hides his illuminated life of St. Patrick and his poem about a cat.

**Sutcliff, Rosemary**
*Blood Feud*
[Scandinavia to Constantinople (Istanbul)]
Dutton 1977
Grades 6–8

In tenth-century Europe two young men try to arrange the murder of their father.

**Sutcliff, Rosemary**
*Dawn Wind*
[United Kingdom (England)]
Walck 1962
Grades 8–10

After a battle with the Saxons a boy is orphaned and travels to northern Britain where he settles.

**Sutcliff, Rosemary**
*The Lantern Bearers*
[United Kingdom (England)]
Walck 1959
Grades 9–12

The Saxons invade Roman Britain and when their galleys left Britain, the hero decided to remain.

**Sutcliff, Rosemary**
*The Shining Company*
[United Kingdom (England)]
Farrar 1990
Grades 9–12

Based on fact the novel recreates the fight between the Three Hundred Champions and the

Saxon invaders in eighth-century Britain.

**Trease, Geoffrey**
*Escape to King Alfred*
[United Kingdom (England)]
Vanguard 1958
Grades 6–8
 This is a fictionalized account of Alfred, King of England from 849–901.

**Treece, Henry**
*Man with A Sword*
[Scandinavia to England]
Oxford 1979
Grades 8–10
 When William the Conqueror was King of England a professional soldier comes to realize that the world he knew was changing and disappearing quickly.

**Treece, Henry**
*The Road to Miklagard*
[Scandinavia to (Constantinople) Istanbul, Turkey]
Criterion 1957
Grades 7–9
 A Viking travels to and from Constantinople.

**Treece, Henry**
*Viking's Dawn*
[Scandinavia to United Kingdom (British Isles)]
Criterion 1956
Grades 7–9
 A Viking boy sails on a Norse ship to seek his fortune.

---

# 1067–1499

**Baumann, Hans (Trans. by Isabel and Florence McHugh)**
*Sons of the Steppe*
[Mongolia]
Walck 1961

Grades 5–7
 This is the story of two of Genghis Khan's grandsons—one becomes a warrior and the other Emperor of the Middle Kingdom.

**Benchley, Nathaniel**
*Beyond the Mists*
[Scandinavia to Greenland and Vineland (Newfoundland/Labrador)]
Harper 1975
Grades 6–9
 An eleventh-century Norseman becomes involved with Leif Eriksson and his explorations.

**Bosse, Malcolm**
*Captives of Time*
[United Kingdom (England)]
Dell 1989
Grades 7–10
 In the medieval world Anne and her brother live with an uncle who is secretly designing the first clock.

**Carson, Dale**
*The Beggar King of China*
[China]
Atheneum 1971
Grades 6–9
 In the Mongol empire of the fourteenth-century, the son of a poor farmer unites the bandit groups to drive the enemy back into Mongolia. This boy becomes the founder of the Ming Dynasty.

**Chute, Marchette**
*The Innocent Wayfaring*
[United Kingdom (England)]
Dutton 1955
Grades 6–8
 When a girl runs away from her convent school, her adventures provide the reader with a good look at fourteenth-century life.

**de Angeli, Marguerite**
*The Door in the Wall*
[United Kingdom (England)]

Doubleday 1949
Grades 5–7

In London during the Middle Ages, at the time of the plague, Robin is separated from his parents and goes to live in a monastery.

**de Travino, Elizabeth**
*Casilda of the Rising Moon*
[Spain]
Farrar 1967
Grades 9–12

This is fictionalized account of the rise of a saint in medieval Spain.

**Doherty, P. C.**
*The Death of a King*
[United Kingdom (England)]
Bantam 1987
Grades 9–12

The story concerns the investigation of the murder of King Edward II in the thirteenth century.

**Gray, Elizabeth Janet**
*Adam of the Road*
[United Kingdom (England)]
Viking 1942
Grades 6–9

A thirteenth-century minstrel boy searches throughout England for his father and his dog.

**Harnett, Cynthia**
*The Merchant's Mark*
[United Kingdom (England)]
Lerner 1984 [1973]
Grades 6–8

In 1493 the son of a wealthy wool merchant uncovers a plot to ruin his father's business.

**Harnett, Cynthia**
*The Writing on the Hearth*
[United Kingdom (England)]
Lerner 1984
Grades 8–10

The stepson of a plowman wants to go to Oxford but finds that witchcraft and politics stand in his way.

**Haugaard, Erik**
*Leif the Unlucky*
[Greenland]
Houghton 1982
Grades 7–12

The story is a fictionalized account of the last remnants of the Greenland colony in the early fifteenth century.

**Hodges, Walter C.**
*Columbus Sails*
[Spain]
Coward-McCann 1939
Grades 3–5

The voyage of Columbus is seen through the eyes of a monk, a sailor, and an Indian who returned with Columbus to Spain.

**Holland, Cecelia**
*The Lords of Vaumartin*
[France]
Houghton 1968
Grades 9–12

This is the story of a 14-year-old misfit in fourteenth-century France.

**Kelly, Eric P.**
*The Trumpeter of Krakow*
[Poland]
Macmillan 1928
Grades 5–8

Set in the fifteenth century, this story is about a jewel and a young patriot who guards it in a church tower.

**Konigsburg, E. L.**
*A Proud Taste for Scarlet and Miniver*
[France and England]
Atheneum 1973
Grades 6–9

Through the eyes of people who knew her, the reader comes to know and understand Eleanor of Aquitaine.

Konigsburg, E. L.
*The Second Mrs. Giaconda*
[Italy]
Atheneum 1975
Grades 6–9

Using a series of invented incidental events, the author tells the story of Leonardo daVinci, his apprentice, and the Mona Lisa.

Mills, Lois
*So Young A Queen*
[Poland]
Lothrop 1960
Grades 5–9

This is a fictionalized account of Jadwiga who ruled Poland in the late 1300s.

Myers, Walter Dean
*The Legend of Tarik*
[Africa]
Scholastic 1982
Grades 7–9

This is an epic medieval novel in which Tarik witnesses the destruction of his people and prepares to avenge them.

O'Dell, Scott
*The Road to Damietta*
[Italy]
Fawcett 1987
Grades 8–12

In the thirteenth century Francis Bernadone turns from a playboy to become St. Francis of Assisi.

Paterson, Katherine
*Of Nightingales That Weep*
[Japan]
Crowell 1974
Grades 7–9

The daughter of a famous samurai killed during the civil wars becomes a court musician as well as a personal servant and must deal with her clashing loyalties.

Paterson, Katherine
*The Sign of the Chrysanthemum*
[Japan]
Crowell 1973
Grades 7–10

In feudal Kyoto a young boy searches for his samurai father during the twelfth century civil wars.

Paton Walsh, Jill
*The Emperor's Winding Sheet*
[Constantinople (Istanbul)]
Farrar 1974
Grades 7–9

The siege and fall of Constantinople (Istanbul), Turkey, is seen through the eyes of a British seaman who is first a prisoner of Emperor Constantine and later his devoted servant.

Picard, Barbara
*One Is One*
[United Kingdom (England)]
Holt 1966
Grades 9–12

The son of a great nobleman is a misfit because of his introspective nature, artistic bent, and fear of dogs—and so he is sent to live in a monastery.

Sancha, Sheila Walter
*Dragun's Town*
[United Kingdom (England)]
Crowell 1989
Grades 4–7

Based of information from the Hundred Rolls of 1275, the author gives an account of one summer in the town of Stanford.

Skurzynski, Gloria
*Manwolf*
[Poland]
Houghton 1981
Grades 9–12

A medieval adolescent boy is thought to be a werewolf.

**Skurzynski, Gloria**
*The Minstrel in the Tower*
[France]
Random 1988
Grades 3–5

Two children set out to find their unknown uncle when their father does not return from the Crusades.

**Skurzynski, Gloria**
*What Happened in Hamlin*
[Germany]
Four Winds 1979
Grades 6–8

By way of an orphan boy a reasonable explanation is given for the disappearance of the children of Hamlin.

**Stevenson, Robert Louis**
*The Black Arrow*
[United Kingdom (England)]
Scribner 1987
Grades 7–12

A boy becomes involved in the War of the Roses when he fights to regain his inheritance.

**Sutcliff, Rosemary**
*Knight's Fee*
[United Kingdom (England)]
Walck 1960
Grades 5–7

A boy who is keeper of the hounds of Arundel Castle eventually becomes a knight.

**Sutcliff, Rosemary**
*The Shield Ring*
[United Kingdom (England)]
Walck 1972 [1957]
Grades 7–9

In the eleventh century a girl becomes aware of the fading power of the Norse in their final conflict with the Normans.

**Sutcliff, Rosemary**
*The Witch's Brat*

[United Kingdom (England)]
Walck 1970
Grades 7–9

This is a fictionalized account of the founding of St. Bartholomew's Hospital and the story of an orphan boy who is cast out of the community that raised him.

**Trease, Geoffrey**
*The Baron's Hostage*
[United Kingdom (England)]
Nelson 1975 [1952]
Grades 6–8

The lives of a teenage boy and girl become intertwined when the former lays claim to a barony and the latter must deal with an arranged marriage.

**Trease, Geoffrey**
*Bows against the Barons*
[United Kingdom (England)]
Meredith 1967 [1934]
Grades 6–8

A peasant boy joins Robin Hood and his men when he carelessly kills one of the king's deer.

**Trease, Geoffrey**
*The Red Towers of Granada*
[England and Spain]
Vanguard 1967
Grades 6–10

Robin leaves England with the Jewish doctor who diagnosed his skin disease as a minor ailment, not leprosy as the villagers who cast him out thought.

**Treece, Henry**
*The Last Viking*
[United Kingdom (England) and Scandinavia]
Pantheon 1966
Grades 7–9

This is a fictionalized account of Harold Hardrada who was the last Viking leader and King of Norway.

**Treece, Henry**
*Perilous Pilgrimage*
[France and Morocco]
Criterion 1959
Grades 8–10

Two children angered at their father's remarriage, follow the shepherd boy, Stephen of Cloyes, who assembled an army of children to make a crusade to the Holy Land only to be sold into slavery.

**Turner, Ann**
*The Way Home*
[United Kingdom (England)]
Crown 1982
Grades 6–9

During the plague a young girl who is persecuted because of a harelip runs away and hides in the marshes. She has to fend for herself until it is safe to come home.

**Voigt, Cynthia**
*Jackaroo*
[Europe]
Atheneum 1985
Grades 7–9

The daughter of an innkeeper comes to aid of poor tenants.

**Voigt, Cynthia**
*On Fortune's Wheel*
[Europe]
Atheneum 1990
Grades 6–8

In the same medieval world of *Jackaroo* another innkeeper's daughter, two generations later, struggles with society's expectations for her.

**Welch, Ronald**
*Bowman of Crecy*
[England and France]
Criterion 1967
Grades 8–10

In the fourteenth century the head of an outlaw gang enters the service of a knight to fight for king and country.

**Willard, Barbara**
*The Miller's Boy*
[United Kingdom (England)]
Dutton 1976
Grades 6–8

In fifteenth-century Sussex the sons of a miller and landowner become close friends but when they grow up their friendship disintegrates because of class distinctions.

## 1500–1699

**Beatty, John and Patricia**
*Holdfast*
[United Kingdom (England)]
Morrow 1972
Grades 4–6

At the time of Elizabeth I an Irish orphan is captured and taken to England.

**Beatty, John and Patricia**
*King's Knight's Pawn*
[United Kingdom (England) and Ireland (Eire)]
Morrow 1971
Grades 7–9

A 14-year-old boy sees Charles I beheaded and runs away to Ireland where he becomes involved in events that lead to the Roundhead Massacre of the Irish.

**Beatty, John and Patricia**
*Pirate Royal*
[American Colonies and England]
Morrow 1969
Grades 8–10

A boy is falsely accused of theft, put in prison, sold as a handservant, and then joins Henry Morgan's band of pirates. Eventually, the King of England pardons him.

**Beatty, John and Patricia**
*Witch Dog*
[United Kingdom (England)]

Morrow 1968
Grades 6–8

Prince Rupert leads the King's cavalry in the Civil War.

**Bulla, Clyde Robert and Michael Syson**
*Conquista!*
[Mexico]
Crowell 1968
Grades 2–5

A horse wanders away from Coronado's expedition that was searching for the "city of gold," and is found by an Indian boy who has never seen a horse.

**Burton, Hester**
*Beyond the Weir Bridge*
[United Kingdom (England)]
Crowell 1970
Grades 7–9

Three youngsters remain friends despite religious and political differences, the plague, and rivalry in love.

**Burton, Hester**
*Kate Ryder*
[United Kingdom (England)]
Crowell 1975
Grades 8–10

In 1646 an English girl tries to cope with divided loyalties during the Civil War.

**Cheetham, Ann**
*The Pit*
[United Kingdom (England)]
Holt 1990
Grades 4–8

A boy living in a centuries-old house is drawn back to the London of 1665 where he enters the body of a child who, with his family, had to stay in this house until they all died of the plague.

**Chute, Marchette**
*The Wonderful Winter*
[United Kingdom (England)]

Dutton 195
Grades 6–8

A boy runs away to London to play bit parts on the Elizabethan stage and mixes with the theater crowd.

**de Trevino, Elizabeth Borton**
*I, Juan de Pareja*
[Spain]
Farrar 1965
Grades 7–12

Juan is a slave who serves the painter Velasquez and secretly and illegally becomes a painter on his own. On confessing this to the king, his master frees him.

**Dunlop, Eileen**
*The Valley of the Deer*
[United Kingdom (Scotland)]
Holiday 1989
Grades 5–8

A girl and her archaeologist parents move to the Valley of the Deer where Anne finds a Bible from the 1600s. It leads her in a hunt of her own that sends her back to the seventeenth century and its witchcraft trials.

**Griffiths, Helen**
*The Mysterious Appearance of Agnes*
[Germany]
Holiday 1975
Grades 6–8

A young girl is accused of witchcraft.

**Harnett, Cynthia**
*The Great House*
[United Kingdom (England)]
Lerner 1984 [1949]
Grades 6–8

In the late seventeenth century two children go with their architect father to a country estate where he builds a modern house.

**Harnett, Cynthia**
*Stars of Fortune*
[United Kingdom (England)]
Lerner 1984 [1956]
Grades 7–9

In 1554 four children who are ancestors of George Washington become involved in a plan to free Princess Elizabeth who is held captive in a nearby castle.

**Haugaard, Erik C.**
*Cromwell's Boy*
[United Kingdom (England)]
Houghton 1978
Grades 6–8

A 13-year-old boy fights with Cromwell against King Charles.

**Haugaard, Erik C.**
*A Messenger for Parliament*
[United Kingdom (England)]
Houghton 1976
Grades 8–10

In 1685 an old Bostonian man recalls his part in the English Civil War when he joined a rag-tag group of children who followed the English Parliamentary Army.

**Haugaard, Erik C.**
*The Samurai's Tale*
[Japan]
Houghton 1984
Grades 9–12

In the sixteenth century an orphaned boy is looked after by a general who serves a great warlord and ends up as a samurai for the enemies of his dead family.

**Haugaard, Erik C.**
*The Untold Tale*
[Denmark]
Houghton 1971
Grades 8–10

A Danish orphan seeks his fortune during the wars with Sweden.

**Highwater, Jamake**
*The Sun, He Dies*
[Mexico]
Meridian 1984
Grades 9–12

Cortez searches for gold and fame and destroys the Aztec civilization.

**Hunter, Mollie**
*The Ghosts of Glencoe*
[United Kingdom (Scotland)]
Funk and Wagnalls 1969
Grades 8–10

A young officer tells of the Massacre at Glencoe where the King's soldiers and Highland clansmen fought.

**Hunter, Mollie**
*The Spanish Letters*
[United Kingdom (Scotland)]
Funk and Wagnalls 1967
Grades 8–10

Two Spanish agents are allied with Scottish traitors who are planning to kidnap King James.

**Hunter, Mollie**
*You Never Knew Her as I Did*
[United Kingdom (Scotland)]
Harper 1981
Grades 7–9

A 17-year-old boy tries to help Mary, Queen of Scots, escape.

**Ish-Kishor, Sulamith**
*A Boy of Old Prague*
[Czechoslovakia]
Scholastic 1980 [1963]
Grades 5–8

In the 1500s a peasant boy grows up in the Jewish ghetto of Prague.

**Lewis, Mildred D.**
*The Honorable Sword*
[Japan]
Houghton 1960

Grades 4–8

This story is set in sixteenth-century Japan and clearly depicts the fight between clans for power and a shogunate government that is trying to unify the country.

**McGraw, Eloise**
*Master Cornhill*
[United Kingdom (England)]
Atheneum 1973
Grades 6–9

A boy finds himself without friends, family, and money when the plague and Great Fire hit London.

**Minard, Rosemary Long**
*Meg*
[England and France]
Pantheon 1982
Grades 3–6

Disguised as a man, a young girl joins Henry VIII's army fighting in France.

**Namioka, Lensey**
*The Samurai and the Long-Nosed Devils*
[Japan]
McKay 1976
Grades 6–9

In sixteenth-century Japan two *ronin* become the bodyguards of Portuguese missionaries. The reader experiences the clash of two cultures from the Japanese point of view.

**Namioka, Lensey**
*Valley of the Broken Cherry Trees*
[Japan]
Delacorte 1980
Grades 4–6

Two sixteenth-century samurai get involved in conspiracies.

**O'Dell, Scott**
*The Amethyst Ring*
[Mexico (Yucatan)]
Houghton 1983
Grades 7–10

The *conquistadores* ravage the Mayans.

**O'Dell, Scott**
*The Captive*
[Spain and Mexico]
Houghton 1979
Grades 7–10

In sixteenth-century Spain a young seminarian is pressed into a voyage to the New World. He is shocked by the practice of Indian enslavement, their harsh treatment, and the taking of their gold. After a shipwreck he is helped by a Mayan girl.

**O'Dell, Scott**
*The Feathered Serpent*
[Mexico]
Houghton 1981
Grades 7–10

Julian, shipwrecked in *The Captive,* is now the god Kukulcan. The story, which is set in the Mayan world, centers on the meeting of Montezuma and Cortés.

**O'Dell, Scott**
*The King's Fifth*
[Mexico (Yucatan)]
Houghton 1966
Grades 6–9

Estaban, a young mapmaker, is diverted from his search for knowledge by his desire for gold.

**Paton Walsh, Jill**
*A Parcel of Patterns*
[United Kingdom (England)]
Farrar 1983
Grades 9–12

In 1660 a parcel is sent from London to a journeyman tailor and plague is brought to an English village.

**Pope, Elizabeth Marie**
*The Perilous Gard*
[United Kingdom (England)]
Hall 1976
Grades 6–8

A girl is banished from Princess Elizabeth's castle and is sent to a distant castle.

**Richemont, Enid**
*The Time Tree*
[United Kingdom (England)]
Little 1990
Grades 4–6

The differences between life in Elizabethan England and today are clearly drawn in this time fantasy when two girls meet a deaf child from Elizabethan times while playing in their tree house.

**Stolz, Mary**
*Bartholomew Fair*
[United Kingdom (England)]
Greenwillow 1990
Grades 5–8

In 1597 six people from different walks of life find that their paths cross at Bartholomew Fair.

**Stone, Irving**
*The Agony and the Ecstasy*
[Italy]
Signet 1987 [1961]
Grades 10–12

This is a fictionalized account of Michelangelo and his times.

**Sutcliff, Rosemary**
*Bonnie Dundee*
[United Kingdom (Scotland)]
Dutton 1984
Grades 9–12

A man remembers his youth as a follower of Bonnie Dundee who tried to win back Scotland for the Catholic King James.

**Van Canon, Claudia**
*The Inheritance*
[Spain]
Houghton 1983
Grades 9–12

During the Inquisition in the sixteenth century, a young medical student experiences the horrors of the time.

**Vining, Elizabeth Gray**
*I Will Adventure*
[United Kingdom (England)]
Viking 1962
Grades 5–7

In 1596 a boy goes to London to be a page to his uncle, sees *Romeo and Juliet*, and meets Master Burbage and the Bard himself.

**Willard, Barbara**
*The Mantlemass Chronicles*
[United Kingdom (England)]

(This is a series of seven books set during the sixteenth and seventeenth centuries that trace the conflicts of the Malloy family through several generations.)

———.
*The Lark and the Laurel*
Dell 1989 [1970]
Grades 9–12

A Tudor king is on the throne and 16-year-old Cecily is sent to live at the manor.

———.
*The Sprig of Broom*
Dell 1989 [1972]
Grades 9–12

A young man, Piers, has to settle the question of his parentage in order to marry Cecily.

———.
*A Cold Wind Blowing*
Dell 1989 [1973]
Grades 9–12

Piers has to deal with the Reformation of Henry VIII—a time when nuns were burned as witches and monasteries were dismantled.

———.
*The Eldest Son*
Dell 1989 [1977]

Grades 9–12

Harry wants to be master of Ghylls Hatch but disdains the horses that are its splendor and wants to turn the place into a forge.

_____.
*The Iron Lily*
Dell 1989 [1974]
Grades 9–12

Lilias no longer has a place in the house when her mother dies and she has to live on her own.

_____.
*A Flight of Swans*
Dell 1989 [1980]
Grades 9–12

The selfishness of traitors becomes evident when the Spanish Armada sails for England.

_____.
*Harrow and Harvest*
Dell 1989 [1975]
Grades 9–12

Families are split when king and Parliament are at odds.

# 1700–1799

Almedingen, E. M.
*Anna*
[Russia]
Farrar 1972
Grades 7–10

This is a story of life in eighteenth- and nineteenth-century Czarist Russia.

Almedingen, E. M.
*The Crimson Oak*
[Russia]
Coward-McCann 1983
Grades 7–10

A boy grows up in Czarist Russia.

Almedingen, E.M.
*Young Mark*
[Russia, Ukraine]
Farrar 1967
Grades 6–8

In the eighteenth century a Ukranian boy leaves his home and travels to St. Petersburg to become a singer.

Beatty, John and Patricia
*The Royal Dirk*
[United Kingdom (Scotland)]
Morrow 1966
Grades 6–8

Bonnie Prince Charlie is entrusted to a young man to guide the prince's party through the hills to escape the English armies.

Bond, Nancy
*Another Shore*
[Canada]
McElderry 1988
Grades 7–10

A mother and daughter spend a summer together in Nova Scotia working for Parks Canada in the reconstructed 1744 Port of Louisbourg. The 17-year-old daughter finds herself thrown back to the year when she is accepted as a member of a large family that owns a bakery.

Burton, Hester
*To Ravensrigg*
[United Kingdom (England)]
Crowell 1977
Grades 8–10

Looking for her real father, a girl is led to Liverpool and its slave trade.

Burton, Hester
*The Rebel*
[United Kingdom (England)]
Crowell 1972
Grades 7–9

An English student who champions freedom is disillusioned by the French Revolution.

**Burton, Hester**
*Riders of the Storm*
[United Kingdom (England)]
Crowell 1973
Grades 10–12
 A teacher in a slum school in Manchester in the 1700s is charged with conspiracy.

**Calvert, Patricia**
*Hadder McColl*
[United Kingdom (Scotland)]
Scribner 1985
Grades 7–9
 A 15-year-old Highland girl cannot understand why her brother, on his return from school in Edinburgh, is no longer interested in the Jacobite cause.

**Chauncy, Nan**
*Hunted in Their Own Land*
[Australia]
Seabury 1973
Grades 7–12
 The Aborigines of Tasmania are annihilated by the whites.

**Clark, Ann Nolan**
*Secret of the Andes*
[Peru]
Viking 1952
Grades 4–8
 An Inca boy who tends a herd of llamas in the mountains decides to leave his valley and go down to the world of the Spanish people.

**Dickens, Charles**
*A Tale of Two Cities*
[United Kingdom (England) and France]
Silver 1985 [1859]
Grades 9–12
 The lives of ordinary people are greatly changed during the French Revolution.

**Garfield, Leon**
*The Apprentices*
[United Kingdom (England)]
Penguin 1988 [1978]
Grades 7–10
 Twelve stories about apprentices in eighteenth century London re-create the sights, sounds, smells, and customs of the time.

**Garfield, Leon**
*Black Jack*
[United Kingdom (England)]
Longman 1968
Grades 8–10
 A London apprentice becomes involved with a criminal and a "mad" girl.

**Garfield, Leon**
*The Boy and the Monkey*
[United Kingdom (England)]
Watts 1969
Grades 5–7
 An orphaned boy trains his monkey to steal for him, the penalty for which is hanging.

**Garfield, Leon**
*Devil in the Fog*
[United Kingdom (England)]
Dell 1988 [1966]
Grades 4–6
 A 14-year-old boy finds out he is the son of a rich and powerful man and then becomes part of this world.

**Garfield, Leon**
*Drummer Boy*
[France and United Kingdom (England)]
Pantheon 1969
Grades 7–9
 After their regiment is defeated in France, a drummer boy and six other survivors manage to return to England.

**Garfield, Leon**
*The Empty Sleeve*
[United Kingdom (England)]
Delacorte 1988

Grades 4–6

Twin boys come to grips with their destinies after one is apprenticed to a locksmith and finds himself in great danger.

**Garfield, Leon**
*Footsteps*
[United Kingdom (England)]
Dell 1988
Grades 4–6

When his father dies, a 12-year-old boy goes to London.

**Garfield, Leon**
*Smith*
[United Kingdom (England)]
Dell 1987 [1967]
Grades 2–6

Eighteenth-century London is seen through the eyes of a pickpocket.

**Garfield, Leon**
*The Sound of Coaches*
[United Kingdom (England)]
Viking 1974
Grades 9–12

A boy is taken in as a foster son by the couple who was driving the coach in which his mother was riding when she died. After carelessly wrecking the coach, he is cast out, goes to London, and finds a new and adventurous life.

**Harris, Christie**
*Raven's Cry*
[Canada]
Atheneum 1966
Grades 9–12

In 1775 the white men came to the Haida people to hunt sea otters and destroy their way of life.

**Haugaard, Erik C.**
*A Boy's Will*
[United Kingdom (England)]
Houghton 1983

Grades 6–8

A boy defies his smuggler grandfather and notifies John Paul Jones about an English ambush.

**Hendry, Frances**
*Quest for a Kelpie*
[United Kingdom (Scotland)]
Holiday 1988
Grades 6–8

Scottish Highlanders rebel against the English king and the village is caught in the war.

**Hunter, Mollie**
*The Lothian Run*
[United Kingdom (Scotland)]
Funk and Wagnalls 1970
Grades 8–10

In 1736 a lawyer's clerk is involved with smuggling.

**O'Dell, Scott**
*My Name is Not Angelica*
[Africa and the Virgin Islands]
Houghton 1989
Grades 6–8

An African girl is sold into slavery by another tribe and is sent to Danish planters in the Virgin Islands.

**Orczy, Baronus**
*The Scarlet Pimpernel*
[France]
Signet 1974 [1905]
Grades 9–12

An English nobleman disguises himself and saves members of the French royalty from the Reign of Terror during the French Revolution.

**Paterson, Katherine**
*The Master Puppeteer*
[Japan]
Crowell 1976
Grades 7–9

In eighteenth-century Osaka, when Japan's old samurai tradition was dying, a boy runs away from home to apprentice himself to the Hanaza puppet theater.

**Roberts, Margaret**
*Stephanie's Children*
[France]
Victor Gollancz 1969
Grades 7–9
   During the French Revolution the Reign of Terror affects individuals and families.

**Stevenson, Robert Louis**
*Kidnapped*
[United Kingdom (Scotland)]
Scribner 1982 [1886]
Grades 7–12
   These are the memoirs of David Balfour, set in 1751 in the Highlands, that tell the story of his exploits with the reckless Alan Breck.

**Trease, Geoffrey**
*Victory at Valmy*
[France]
Vanguard 1960
Grades 5–7
   A starving, artistic boy is taken under the wing of an eccentric woman who is at home with nobility and revolutionaries.

## 1800–1899

**Achebe, Chinua**
*Things Fall Apart*
[Nigeria]
Fawcett 1985 [1959]
Grades 9–12
   This is the shocking story about a member of the Obi Tribe in Africa when white people come to the village.

**Aiken, Joan**
*The Truth of the Gale*
[Spain]

Harper 1988
Grades 7–9
   A boy and his friends are asked to rescue three kidnapped children during the 1820s revolution.

**Allan, Mabel Foster**
*The Mills down Below*
[United Kingdom (England)]
Dodd 1981
Grades 6–9
   The story takes place in Victorian times and the reader is given an excellent insight into industrialization.

**Almedingen, E. M.**
*Katia*
[Russia]
Farrar 1966
Grades 5–7
   This an adaptation of the memoirs of the author's great-aunt that were published in Russia in 1874.

**Avery, Gillian**
*A Likely Lad*
[United Kingdom (England)]
Holt 1971
Grades 6–8
   A nineteenth-century boy runs away from Manchester because his father pressures him to enter a career he does not want.

**Bartos-Hoppner, B.**
*Storm over the Caucasus*
[Russia]
Walck 1968
Grades 9–12
   A shepherd boy joins the men of Caucasian tribes under the leadership of Imam Shamyl to fight against Russian domination.

**Beatty, Patricia**
*Jonathan down Under*
[Australia]
Morrow 1982

Grades 5–7

A 13-year-old boy goes with his gold miner father to Australia.

**Bunting, Eve**
*The Haunting of Kildoran Abbey*
[Ireland]
Warne 1978
Grades 6–8

A gang of foundlings struggle to survive during the 1847 famine.

**Burton, Hester**
*The Henchmens at Home*
[United Kingdom (England)]
Oxford 1970
Grades 6–8

Three children grow up in Victorian times.

**Burton, Hester**
*No Beat of Drum*
[England and Australia]
World 1967
Grades 9–12

Two boys and a girl are convicted of minor crimes and are sent to a penal colony in Tasmania.

**Burton, Hester**
*Time of Trial*
[United Kingdom (England)]
Collins-World 1964
Grades 9–12

A girl tells about her life in London during the early 1800s and focuses on the poor and unfair justice system.

**Cameron, Eleanor**
*The Court of the Stone Children*
[France]
Dutton 1973
Grades 5–7

With the help of a journal written by a woman in the 1800s, a girl solves a murder mystery from Napoleon's time.

**Carter, Peter**
*The Black Lamp*
[United Kingdom (England)]
Nelson, 1973
Grades 9–12

In 1819 the son of a weaver becomes involved in the fight of the weavers against the mill owners who are bringing in machine-driven looms.

**Coatsworth, Elizabeth**
*Jon the Unlucky*
[Greenland]
Holt 1964
Grades 4–7

A 9-year-old orphaned Dane finds the hidden valley where the descendants of Lief the Lucky lived and takes the place of the last scholar in the valley.

**Conlon-McKenna, Marita**
*Under the Hawthorne Tree*
[Ireland]
Holiday 1990
Grades 4–7

At the time of the famine in the 1840s, three children whose mother left to find their father are dispossessed and sent to the workhouse. They escape and are left to fend for themselves.

**Dickens, Charles**
*Great Expectations*
[United Kingdom (England)]
Bantam 1986 [1861]
Grades 7–12

Pip comes of age in the refined but corrupt Victorian world.

**Dickens, Charles**
*Hard Times*
[United Kingdom (England)]
Bantam 1988 [1854]
Grades 7–12

The novel deals with the callousness of Victorian England's industrial and educational systems.

**Gaan, Margaret**
*Red Barbarians*
[China]
Dodd 1989
Grades 9–12
  This is a tale of love and smuggling.

**Garfield, Leon**
*Night of the Comet*
[United Kingdom (England)]
Dell 1988 [1979]
Grades 4–6
  This is a complicated comedy that involves three couples of star-crossed lovers.

**Garfield, Leon**
*Young Nick and Jubilee*
[United Kingdom (England)]
Doubleday 1989
Grades 4–6
  In 1850 two orphans run away to London and their lives improve when they meet a pickpocket and a student from a charity school.

**Harris, Christie**
*Forbidden Frontier*
[Canada]
Atheneum 1968
Grades 7–12
  The Haida Indians are badly treated by white fur traders.

**Hodges, Walter C.**
*The Overland Launch*
[United Kingdom (England)]
Coward-McCann 1970
Grades 6–8
  On January 12, 1899, a storm does not permit the launching of the Lynmouth lifeboat so the crew takes it thirteen miles overland.

**Hunter, Mollie**
*A Pistol in Greenyards*
[United Kingdom (Scotland)]
Funk and Wagnalls 1968

Grades 8–10
  In 1854 a boy tries to stop the eviction of his family from their farm.

**Lampedusa, Giuseppe di**
*The Leopard*
[Italy]
Pantheon 1987 [1960]
Grades 9–12
  A Sicilian lord reacts to Garibaldi and laments the passing of a way of life that he loved and enjoyed.

**Langford, Sondra Gordon**
*Red Bird of Ireland*
[Ireland]
Macmillan 1983
Grades 6–8
  A 13-year-old boy survives the 1846 potato famine.

**Monjo, F. N.**
*Prisoners of the Scrambling Dragon*
[China]
Holt 1980
Grades 4–7
  Smugglers board a Yankee trading ship and a cabin boy and his friend, an escaped slave, find themselves sailing with opium pirates.

**Musil, Robert (Trans. by Eithne Wilkins and Ernst Kaiser)**
*Young Torless*
[Austria]
Pantheon 1982 [1955]
Grades 9–12
  This is the story of the discovery of physical, emotional, and sexual power in an Austrian military boarding school at the time of the Hapsburgs.

**Parker, F. M.**
*The Slavers*
[Mexico]
New American Library 1990
Grades 9–12

A young man runs away from the terror of Zaldivar, Mexico's most powerful war chief, and finds refuge in a polygamous colony that is constantly raided by Zaldivar for its women. The price of his freedom is Zaldivar's death.

Paterson, Katherine
*Rebels of the Heavenly Kingdom*
[Japan]
Dutton 1983
Grades 7–9

Two young people become involved in the Taiping Rebellion of 1850. A comparison can be made to modern cults.

Paton Walsh, Jill
*A Chance Child*
[United Kingdom (England)]
Farrar 1978
Grades 8–10

In 1833 a boy looks for his mistreated half-brother who escaped from a locked closet and joins other mistreated children who were victims of the Industrial Revolution.

Patton Walsh, Jill
*The Huffler*
[United Kingdom (England)]
Farrar 1975
Grades 6–8

Late in the nineteenth century a girl joins the crew of a canal boat.

Peyton, K. M.
*Dear Fred*
[United Kingdom (England)]
Philomel 1981
Grades 10–12

In the 1880s a girl falls in love with a jockey in the racing world of Newmarket.

Peyton, K. M.
*The Maplin Bird*
[United Kingdom (England)]
World 1965

Grades 9–12

Two sibling orphans run away from an abusive aunt and uncle and make their own way in the world.

Peyton, K. M.
*The Right-hand Man*
[United Kingdom (England)]
Oxford 1977
Grades 9–12

In 1818 a 20-year-old man accepts the job as right-hand man to a lord in order to help him save his estate from a greedy cousin.

Pullman, Phillip
*The Ruby in the Smoke*
[United Kingdom (England)]
Knopf 1987
Grades 6–9

Victorian London is the scene for murder and suspense.

Pullman, Phillip
*Shadow in the North*
[United Kingdom (England)]
Knopf 1988
Grades 8–10

A girl faces many dangers as she struggles to become independent.

Robbins, Ruth
*The Emperor and the Drummer Boy*
[France]
Parnassus 1962
Grades 3–6

A drummer boy waits with Napoleon for the return of his friend who is also a drummer boy.

Schlee, Ann
*Ask Me No Questions*
[United Kingdom (England)]
Holt 1982 [1976]
Grades 6–8

A Victorian girl who is sent away from London during the cholera epidemic of 1848 tries to help children in an asylum.

**Schlee, Ann**
*The Consul's Daughter*
[Algeria]
Atheneum 1972
Grades 5–8
    A girl becomes entangled in the British navy's bombardment of Algiers in 1816.

**Stone, Irving**
*The Origin*
[England/South America/Ecuador (Galapagos Islands)]
Signet 1987 [1980]
Grades 9–12
    This is a fictional re-creation of the life and times of Charles Darwin.

**Uchida, Yoshiko**
*Samurai of Gold Hill*
[Japan]
Scribner 1972
Grades 5–8
    When the Shogunate rule of Japan ends, a boy knows he cannot become a samurai and emigrates. The book clearly illustrates the trauma experienced by samurai warriors when denied their high status and the prejudice and discrimination against Japanese immigrants.

**Willard, Barbara**
*Hetty*
[United Kingdom (England)]
Harcourt 1963
Grades 5–7
    A girl grows up in Victorian times.

**Wilson, Barbara Ker**
*Acacia Terrace*
[Australia]
Scholastic 1990
Grades 3–7
    This is the story of a terrace of houses built in the 1860s in Sydney and three generations of

their inhabitants.

**Yep, Laurence**
*Mountain Light*
[China and the United States]
Harper 1985
Grades 7–9
    In 1855 Squeaky Lou leaves China for California and a new life.

**Yep, Laurence**
*The Serpent's Children*
[China]
Harper 1984
Grades 7–9
    A girl tries to help free China from the Manchus and foreign rule.

## 1900–1945

**Aaron, Chester**
*Gideon*
[Poland]
Lippincott 1982
Grades 6–10
    A first-person narrative by a teenage boy who is a member of the resistance describes the pain and misery of Polish Jews in both the Warsaw Ghetto and Treblinka concentration camp.

**Anderson, Margaret J.**
*Journey of the Shadow Bairns*
[Russia]
Scholastic 1980
Grades 5–8
    In 1903 a Scottish girl and her younger brother use the one-way tickets their parents bought before they died and travel to Canada.

**Baer, Edith**
*A Frost in the Night*
[Germany]
Schocken 1988 [1980]

Grades 7–9

A German girl experiences the growing prejudice against Jews as Hitler comes to power.

**Baklanov, Grigory (Trans. by Antonia W. Bouis)**
*Forever Nineteen*
[USSR (Russia)]
Lippincott 1989
Grades 7–9

A young Russian soldier in World War II must deal with his feelings about killing and tries to make some sense out of the confusion of war.

**Ballard, J. G.**
*Empire of the Sun*
[China]
Simon and Schuster 1984
Grades 9–12

A 13-year-old boy in 1939 Shanghai finds his life turned upside down after the Japanese invade. He is separated from his family and put in a prison camp.

**Bartos-Hoppner, B.**
*Hunters of Siberia*
[USSR (Russia)]
Walck 1969
Grades 6–8

A boy and his father, who is the best hunter in their village, are as worried as the other members of their Siberian community because the government is going to limit the hunting of already scarce game.

**Bawden, Nina**
*Carrie's War*
[United Kingdom (Wales)]
Lippincott 1973
Grades 4–7

A mother and her two children are evacuated to a Welsh mining town during the London blitz.

**Benchley, Nathaniel**
*Bright Candles: A Novel of the Danish*

*Resistance*
[Denmark]
Harper 1974
Grades 7–9

A teenage boy fights the Nazis which results in the death of friends, the severance of family ties, and his eventual imprisonment.

**Bishop, Claire Hachet**
*Twenty and Ten*
[France]
Penguin 1984 [1952]
Grades 4–6

Ten young refugees from the Nazis are hidden by a nun and twenty French children.

**Bloch, Marie**
*Aunt America*
[USSR (Ukraine)]
Atheneum 1972 [1963]
Grades 4–7

An American woman visits her niece in a Ukrainian town and the young girl begins to change many of her ideas about life.

**Bloch, Marie**
*Displaced Person*
[USSR (Ukraine)]
Morrow 1978
Grades 6–9

A Ukranian boy escapes from a refugee camp as World War II is about to end.

**Broder, Gloria Kurian and Bill**
*Remember This Time*
[Russia]
New Market (no date)
Grades 9–12

This is the story of a Russian-Jewish family in World War I.

**Buck, Pearl**
*The Big Wave*
[Japan]
Harper 1986 [1948]

Grades 3–6

Two boys growing up in a fishing village have their lives changed by the coming of the big wave.

**Buck, Pearl**
*The Good Earth*
[China]
Oxford 1980 [1931]
Grades 9–12

Life in China is seen through the eyes of one peasant family.

**Burton, Hester**
*In Spite of All Terror*
[United Kingdom (England)]
World 1969
Grades 8–10

A 15-year-old orphan girl is evacuated from the slums of London and sent to live with an aristocratic family in the country.

**Butterworth, Emma Macalik**
*As the Waltz Was Ending*
[Austria]
Four Winds 1985
Grades 7–12

A young dancer lives in Vienna during World War II, during which time the Nazis and then the Russians interrupt her career at the Vienna State Opera.

**Chang, Margaret and Raymond**
*In the Eyes of War*
[China]
McElderry 1990
Grades 4–7

During the final years of World War II, when U.S. planes bomb Shanghai, a boy grasps the significance of his father's involvement in the resistance movement against the Japanese and the threat this posed for the family.

**Collins, Alan**
*Jacob's Ladder*
[Australia]

Lodestar 1989
Grades 7–9

This is a coming of age story about World War II orphans who are sent to a Sydney children's home with other Jewish refugees.

**Cookson, Catherine**
*The Black Candle*
[United Kingdom (England)]
Simon and Schuster 1990
Grades 9–11

In a small village at the turn of the century, families with diverse backgrounds become enmeshed, affecting three generations.

**Cowan, Lore**
*Children of the Resistance*
[Europe]
Hawthorn 1969
Grades 7–12

This is a collection of short stories about youngsters in eight Nazi-occupied countries who sided with the resistance.

**Dank, Milton**
*The Dangerous Game*
[France]
Lippincott 1977
Grades 7–10

A 15-year-old boy who is alone in Paris joins the resistance.

**de Beauvoir, Simone (Trans. by Roger Senhouse and Y. Moyse)**
*The Blood of Others*
[France]
Pantheon 1984 [1948]
Grades 11–12

This book discusses life in Paris during the Nazi occupation.

**De Jong, Meindert**
*The House of Sixty Fathers*
[China]
Harper 1956

Grades 6–9

A boy searches for his parents in Japanese-occupied China during World War II.

**Demetz, Hana**
*The Journey from Prague Street*
[Czechoslovakia]
St. Martin 1990
Grades 7–10

This is the story of a half-Jewish Czech girl during World War II.

**Dickinson, Peter**
*Tulkee*
[China and Tibet]
Dutton 1979
Grades 9–12

A 13-year-old boy escapes from the Boxer Rebellion and travels to Tibet with an English couple. Their lives are changed when they meet a Buddhist monk.

**Doboscq, Genevieve (Trans. by Richard C. Woodward)**
*My Longest Night*
[France]
Seaver 1981
Grades 7–10

D-Day has strong effects on a French family in Normandy.

**Egan, Judith**
*Elena*
[USSR (Russia)]
Ticknor 1981
Grades 10–12

This is a romance set during the Russian Revolution.

**Fenton, Edward**
*The Refugee Summer*
[Greece]
Delacorte 1982
Grades 6–9

A boy from Athens becomes involved in the Graeco-Turkish War of 1922.

**Fife, Dale**
*North of Danger*
[Norway]
Dutton 1978
Grades 5–7

A boy grows up in Norway during World War II.

**Fink, Ida**
*A Scrap of Time: And Other Stories*
[Poland]
Pantheon 1987
Grades 7–10

This is a collection of stories about Polish Jews under the Nazis.

**Follett, Ken**
*The Key to Rebecca*
[Egypt]
Signet 1981
Grades 7–12 ?

A Nazi spy is sent back home to Egypt to gather information from the British and wire it to Rommel who is fighting in the desert.

**Forman, James**
*Ceremony of Innocence*
[Germany]
Farrar 1970
Grades 9–12

Two anti-Nazi students make their thoughts known at the University of Munich in 1942.

**Forman, James**
*Horses of Anger*
[Germany]
Farrar 1967
Grades 9–12

A group of German boys are part of an anti-aircraft battery defending a jet factory with guns whose range is too small to hit U.S. and British planes. Flashbacks cover the whole of World War II.

**Forman, James**
*My Enemy, My Brother*
[Poland and Israel]
Meredith 1969
Grades 7–12

A Jewish family joins the underground but Dan and his grandfather leave the doomed resisters, only to be captured by the Gestapo and sent to a concentration camp. They are ultimately liberated by the Russians and Dan emigrates to Israel.

**Forman, James**
*The Survivor*
[Netherlands (Holland) and Auschwitz
    (Oswiecim, Poland)]
Farrar 1976
Grades 9–12

A Dutch family are victims of the Holocaust and only one person survives.

**Forman, James**
*The Traitors*
[Germany]
Farrar 1968
Grades 9–12

A pastor and his family defy the Nazis and are considered traitors.

**Forster, E. M.**
*Howard's End*
[United Kingdom (England)]
Vintage 1989
Grades 10–12

The novel focuses on the problems between classes in the early 1900s and the eventual accommodations they make.

**Frank, Rudolf (Trans. by Patricia Crampton)**
*No Hero for the Kaiser*
[Poland and Germany]
Lothrop 1986
Grades 7–12

At the beginning of World War I a 14-year-old Polish boy joins the German army and comes to see the horrors of war. Hitler banned this book when he came to power.

**Gardam, Jane**
*A Long Way from Verona*
[United Kingdom (England)]
Macmillan 1988 [1971]
Grades 8–12

A girl who wants to be a writer talks about her experiences, feelings, and perceptions during World War II.

**Garfield, Brian**
*The Paladin*
[United Kingdom (England)]
Bantam 1980
Grades 7–10

During World War II, Winston Churchill recruits a 15-year-old boy to be his personal secret agent.

**Gehrts, Barbara (Trans. by Elizabeth D.
    Crawford)**
*Don't Say a Word*
[Germany]
McElderry 1987
Grades 6–9

An ordinary German family struggles to live under the Nazis whom they loathe.

**Gessner, Lynne**
*Edge of Darkness*
[Latvia]
Walker 1979
Grades 9–12

This is the story of a Latvian farm family during World War II who have lived under three enemy occupations.

**Gleeson, Libby Eleanor**
*Elizabeth*
[Australia]
Holiday 1990
Grades 5–7

When a girl's family moves to her mother's childhood home in western Australia, she finds her grandmother's diary from 1895 and comes to understand life in the bush.

**Griffiths, Helen**
*The Last Summer: Spain 1936*
[Spain]
Holiday 1981
Grades 5–7
   A young boy is caught up in the Spanish civil war.

**Hamori, Laszlo**
*Dangerous Journey*
[Hungary and Austria]
Harcourt 1966
Grades 6–9
   Two boys manage to escape iron curtain Hungary and reach Austria.

**Hartman, Evert**
*War without Friends*
[Holland (Netherlands)]
Crown 1982
Grades 6–8
   In a small Dutch town a 14-year-old boy who is a member of the Hitler Youth is caught between his father's support of the Nazis and his classmates strong opposition to them.

**Haugaard, Eric C.**
*Chase Me, Catch Nobody*
[Denmark and Germany]
Houghton 1980
Grades 5–9
   In 1937 a Danish boy travels into Nazi Germany.

**Hemingway, Ernest**
*A Farewell to Arms*
[Italy]
Macmillan 1987 [1929]
Grades 10–12
   This is a love story that takes place on the Italian front in World War I.

**Hemingway, Ernest**
*For Whom the Bell Tolls*
[Spain]
Macmillan 1988 [1940]
Grades 10–12
   Anti-Fascist guerillas fight in the Spanish civil war.

**Holm, Anne**
*North to Freedom*
[USSR (Russia) and Europe]
Harcourt 1984 [1965]
Grades 6–8
   A boy who grew up in a concentration camp travels across Europe and escapes to freedom.

**Holman, Felice**
*The Wild Children*
[USSR (Russia)]
Scribner 1983
Grades 7–12
   When his family is arrested after the Bolshevik Revolution, a boy joins a group of homeless and despairing wild children who are trying to survive.

**Horgan, Dorothy**
*Then the Zeppelins Came*
[United Kingdom (England)]
Oxford 1990
Grades 5–8
   Two girls from different sides of the track grow up in Edwardian London.

**Hunter, Mollie**
*The Third Eye*
[United Kingdom (Scotland)]
Harper 1979
Grades 9–12
   A girl has the gift of seeing more than meets the eye and herein lies a mystery that involves the laird of the village.

**Hunter, Mollie**
*Sound of Chariots*
[United Kingdom (Scotland)]

**Hall** 1973
Grades 8–10

A girl grows up in poverty in the land of the Firth of Forth.

**Ishiguro, Kazuo**
*An Artist of the Floating World*
[Japan]
Putnam 1986
Grades 9–12

In war-torn Japan an artist tries to deal with changing values.

**Kay, Mara**
*In Face of Danger*
[Germany]
Crown 1977
Grades 6–8

An English girl visiting Germany just before the war finds that her hostess is hiding two Jewish girls in her attic while her son is actively involved in the Hitler Youth.

**Keneally, Thomas**
*Schindler's List*
[Poland, Germany, and Czechoslovakia (Sudetenland)]
Penguin 1982
Grades 9–12

A rich factory owner risks his life and spends his money to save Jews registered as his workers.

**Kerr, Judith**
*When Hitler Stole Pink Rabbit*
[Germany]
Putnam 1972
Grades 4–7

A German-Jewish family escapes from Nazi Germany just before the Nazis arrest the father who is an outspoken journalist and critic of the Nazis.

**Kjerdian, David**
*The Road from Home*
[Armenia (Turkey)]
Penguin 1988

Grades 9–12

A fictionalized biography of the author's mother deals with the persecution and destruction of Armenian Christians by Turkish Moslems.

**Koehn, Ilse Mischling**
*Second Degree*
[Germany]
Greenwillow 1977
Grades 9–12

A woman grows up in Nazi Germany not knowing she is part Jewish.

**Korschunow, Irene (Trans. by Leigh Hafrey)**
*A Night in Distant Motion*
[Germany]
Godine 1983
Grades 7–12

A girl and her parents are loyal, devoted Nazis. When Regine meets a Polish prisoner she realizes the terror of the war and begins to question her beliefs.

**Kotowska, Monika (Trans. by Maia Wojciechowska)**
*The Bridge to the Other Side*
[Europe]
Doubleday 1970
Grades 5–12

This is a collection of short stories, all told in first person, about war orphans during World War II.

**Laird, Christa**
*Shadow of the Wall*
[Poland]
Greenwillow 1990
Grades 7–10

A Jewish boy in the Warsaw Ghetto is involved with Janusz Korczak, a true character, who is considered one of Poland's great heroes.

**Lasenby, Jack**
*The Mangrove Summer*
[New Zealand]
Oxford 1989

Grades 7–9

When the Japanese bomb Pearl Harbor there are fears of an invasion and a boy and his family retreat to an isolated island. His father is a prisoner of war in Germany and the family is terrified by the unending Japanese victories.

**Lasky, Kathryn**
*The Night Journey*
[Russia]
Warne 1981
Grades 4–7

Nana tells her great-granddaughter about Czarist Russia and her eventual escape.

**Levitan, Sonia**
*Journey to America*
[Germany and United States]
Atheneum 1970
Grades 5–8

A mother and three daughters escape from Nazi Germany and travel to the United States to be reunited with the father.

**Lingard, Joan**
*Tug of War*
[Latvia]
Lodestar 1990
Grades 7–9

During World War II two teenagers run away and manage to survive.

**Little, Jean**
*From Anna*
[Germany and Canada]
Harper 1972
Grades 4–6

After escaping from Nazi Germany, a girl and her family must adapt to life in Canada.

**Llewellyn, Richard**
*How Green Was My Valley*
[United Kingdom (Wales)]
Dell 1967 [1940]
Grades 9–12

At the turn of the century the Morgan family, who are miners, gradually see the destruction of the rural countryside.

**Lowry, Lois**
*Number the Stars*
[Denmark]
Houghton 1989
Grades 4–7

A Jewish girl is subjected to Nazi oppression and comes to know the valor of the Danish people.

**Mark, Michael**
*Toba*
[Poland]
Bradbury 1984
Grades 5–7

Through the eyes of a Jewish girl the reader experiences life in a 1910 village.

**Maspero, Francois (Trans. by Nancy Amphoux)**
*Cat's Grin*
[France]
Knopf 1986
Grades 9–12

This is the record of the experiences of a teenager during World War II.

**Matas, Carol**
*Code Name Kris*
[Denmark]
Scribner 1990
Grades 7–12

In this continuation of *Lisa's War* two boys work with the Danish resistance.

**Matas, Carol**
*Lisa's War*
[Denmark]
Scribner 1989
Grades 7–9

The Danish people help Jews to escape.

**Mazer, Harry**
*The Last Mission*
[United States and Germany]
Dell 1981
Grades 7–12
A Jewish-American boy who lied about his age in order to join the air force is imprisoned in a German concentration camp.

**McSwigan, Marie**
*Snow Treasure*
[Norway]
Scholastic 1986 [1942]
Grades 6–9
Young children use sleds to smuggle gold out of Nazi-occupied Norway.

**Moskin, Marietta**
*I Am Rosemarie*
[Germany]
Dell 1987
Grades 6–9
This is a first-person narrative about a girl and her three years in a concentration camp.

**Muhlenweg, Fritz**
*Big Tiger and Christian*
[China]
Pantheon 1952
Grades 6–9
A 12-year-old English boy born in Peking and his Chinese friend become involved in the conflict between war lords in the 1920s.

**Mulisch, Harry (Trans. by Claire White)**
*The Assault*
[Holland (Netherlands)]
Pantheon 1986
Grades 9–12
The Nazis kill an innocent family in retaliation for the assassination of a Dutch collaborator.

**Murray, Michele**
*The Crystal Nights*
[Germany and United States]

Seabury 1973
Grades 6–8
This is a story about the effects of war on its victims and their family in the United States.

**Nostlinger, Christine (Trans. by Anthea Bell)**
*Fly away Home*
[Austria]
Watts 1975
Grades 5–7
A girl remembers what life was like in Vienna at the end of World War II.

**Orgel, Doris**
*The Devil in Vienna*
[Austria]
Dial 1976
Grades 6–8
The best friend of a Jewish girl, whose father is a Nazi and enrolls her in the Hitler Youth, remains loyal to her Jewish friend.

**Orler, Uri**
*The Island on Bird Street*
[Poland]
Houghton 1984
Grades 5–7
A Jewish boy in the Warsaw Ghetto lives in a bombed-out building and experiences fear, loneliness, and starvation rather than surrender to the Nazis.

**Pasternak, Boris**
*Dr. Zhivago*
[USSR (Russia)]
Ballantine 1986 [1958]
Grades 10–12
This is a love story set in Russia at the turbulent time of the Bolshevik Revolution.

**Paton Walsh, Jill**
*The Dolphin Crossing*
[United Kingdom (England)]
St. Martin 1967
Grades 8–10

Two English boys who were too young to fight participate in the evacuation of Dunkirk.

**Paton Walsh, Jill**
*Fireweed*
[United Kingdom (England)]
Farrar 1970
Grades 6–8

Two teenagers who refuse to evacuate from London survive the 1940 blitz.

**Pearson, Kit**
*The Sky is Falling*
[Canada]
Viking 1990
Grades 4–6

During World War II a 10-year-old girl is evacuated to Canada with her 5-year-old brother but she cannot cope with the scars of war.

**Pelgram, Els (Trans. by Maryka and Raphael Rudnik)**
*The Winter when Time Was Frozen*
[Holland (Netherlands)]
Morrow 1980
Grades 6–8

This is the story of a girl and her father at the time of the Allied invasion.

**Peyton, K. M.**
*The Edge of the Cloud*
[United Kingdom (England)]
World 1970
Grades 10–12

A girl helps her boyfriend become a pilot in the early days of aviation.

**Peyton, K. M.**
*Flambards Divided*
[United Kingdom (England)]
Philomel 1982
Grades 10–12

The novel is an addition to the Flambards trilogy and presents a microscopic picture of the new social structure that came out of World War I.

**Peyton, K. M.**
*Thunder in the Sky*
[United Kingdom (England)]
World 1967
Grades 8–10

In 1914 a boy who is too young to enlist sails as a barge hand across the Channel and comes across spies.

**Pople, Maureen**
*The Other Side of the Family*
[Australia]
Knopf 1990
Grades 7–9

A 15-year-old girl is sent to Australia to live with relatives until World War II ends.

**Posell, Elsa**
*Homecoming*
[USSR (Russia)]
Harcourt 1987
Grades 5–8

A Jewish family with six children survives the revolution.

**Ramati, Alexander**
*And the Violins Stopped Playing: A Story of the Gypsy Holocaust*
[Europe]
Watts 1986
Grades 9–12

A young survivor tells of the Nazi slaughter of the Gypsies.

**Raymond, Patrick**
*Daniel and Esther*
[United Kingdom (England)]
McElderry 1990
Grades 7–12

In the shadow of World War II, David, an English boy, and Esther, a Viennese girl, meet at a progressive English school and a strong, sensitive friendship develops.

**Rees, David**
*Exeter Blitz*
[United Kingdom (England)]
Elsevier Nelson 1978
Grades 8–10
  When a bombing raid begins a 14-year-old boy who is on top of the Exeter Cathedral survives and then searches for his family.

**Remarque, Erich M.**
*All Quiet on the Western Front*
[Germany and France]
Barron 1984 [1929]
Grades 9–12
  This book chronicles the experiences of a young German soldier in World War I and vividly portrays the horrors of trench warfare.

**Richter, Hans Peter**
*Friedrich*
[Germany]
Penguin 1987 [1970]
Grades 7–10
  Through a child's eyes the reader comes to know the terror and panic suffered by German Jews.

**Richter, Hans Peter**
*I Was There*
[Germany]
Penguin 1987 [1972]
Grades 6–9
  This is a first-person explanation of the daily lives of young Germans in the Third Reich.

**Roth-Hanno, Renee**
*Touch Wood: A Girlhood in Occupied France*
[France]
Four Winds 1988
Grades 5–7
  Three Jewish girls leave their parents to find asylum in a convent.

**Sachs, Marilyn**
*A Pocket Full of Seeds*
[France]
Doubleday 1973
Grades 5–7
  A French-Jewish family is persecuted by the Nazis.

**Samuels, Gertrude**
*Mottele*
[Poland]
New American Library
Grades 7–10
  A Jewish boy joins the partisans fighting the Nazis.

**Schloneger, Florence**
*Sara's Trek*
[Russia and Poland]
Newton 1981
Grades 5–10
  This is the story of a family of Russian Mennonites who flee to Poland because they trust the Nazis more than the Russians.

**Scholl, Inge (Trans. by Arthur R. Schultz)**
*Students against Tyranny*
[Germany]
Wesleyan 1970
Grades 10–12
  Six young Germans resist the Nazis.

**Sender, Ruth M.**
*The Cage*
[Poland]
Macmillan 1986
Grades 8–12
  A girl is separated from her family and endures the horrors of a concentration camp.

**Seredy, Kate**
*The Good Master*
[Hungary]
Viking 1963 [1935]
Grades 4–6
  A girl lives on her uncle's farm just before World War I and shares farm life with her cousin.

**Serraillier, Ian**
*Escape from Warsaw*
[Poland]
Scholastic 1972 [1958]
Grades 7–9

During World War II three children are separated from their family and try to escape from the war's destruction.

**Sevela, Ephraim**
*We Were Not Like Other People*
[USSR (Russia)]
Harper 1989
Grades 6–9

In 1937 a 9-year-old Jewish boy, whose father was a Red Army Commander and a victim of Stalin's purge, manages to survive.

**Shemin, Margaretha**
*The Little Riders*
[Holland (Netherlands)]
Putnam 1987
Grades 4–6

An American girl is caught in Holland during World War II and helps hide the treasures of the town.

**Steinbeck, John**
*The Moon Is Down*
[Norway]
Penguin 1982 [1942]
Grades 10–12

This story discusses the resistance during World War II.

**Suhl, Yuri**
*Uncle Misha's Partisans*
[Ukraine, USSR]
Four Winds 1973
Grades 5–7

Jewish partisans fight in Ukraine.

**Suhl, Yuri**
*The Other Side of the Gate*
[Poland]

Watts 1975
Grades 7–10

A woman gives birth to a baby in the Warsaw Ghetto after the Nazis outlaw pregnancy and is helped to safety by Christians.

**Szambelan-Strevinski, Christine**
*Dark Hour of Noon*
[Poland]
Lippincott 1982
Grades 5–12

A group of children resist the Nazis and kill an officer who murdered a neighborhood family. They derail trains, bomb cars, and harass the Nazis.

**Takashima, Shican**
*A Child in Prison Camp*
[Canada]
Morrow 1974
Grades 3–6

A fictionalized autobiography depicts the internment of Japanese Canadians during World War II.

**Taylor, Sydney**
*A Papa Like Everyone Else*
[Czechoslovakia]
Dell 1989
Grades 4–6

A Jewish mother and two daughters live on a farm during World War I while the father is in the United States working and saving to send for his family.

**Tene, Benjamin**
*In the Shade of the Chestnut Tree*
[Poland]
Jewish Publication Society 1981
Grades 6–9

Jewish children grow up between the two World Wars.

**Terlouw, Jan**
*Winter in Warsaw*
[Holland (Netherlands)]
McGraw 1976
Grades 6–9
   During World War II a boy takes care of a wounded British flyer.

**Treseder, Terry Walton**
*Hear O Israel*
[Poland]
Atheneum 1990
Grades 3–6
   A 13-year-old boy is getting ready for his Bar Mitzvah in the last days of the Warsaw Ghetto.

**Tunis, John R.**
*His Enemy His Friend*
[France]
Morrow 1967
Grades 7–9
   A German soldier stationed in France is friendly with the French and questions his loyalties.

**Tunis, John R.**
*Silence over Dunkerque*
[France]
Morrow 1962
Grades 7–12
   A British sergeant leads his troops through Dunkerque.

**Van Stockum, Hilda**
*The Borrowed House*
[Germany and Holland (Netherlands)]
Farrar 1975
Grades 7–10
   A girl who is a member of the Hitler Youth joins her German actor parents in Holland (Netherlands) and questions what she was taught.

**Wei, Katherine and Terry Quinn**
*Second Daughter*
[China]
Little 1984

Grades 9–12
   This is a story about growing up in China between 1930 and 1949.

**Westall, Robert**
*Blitzcat*
[United Kingdom (England)]
Scholastic 1989
Grades 9–12
   Through the eyes of an affectionate black cat, the reader sees the devastation of World War II.

**Westall, Robert**
*Fathom Five*
[United Kingdom (England)]
Greenwillow 1979
Grades 8–10
   In 1943 a teenager tries to find a spy.

**Westall, Robert**
*The Machine Gunners*
[United Kingdom (England)]
Random 1990 [1975]
Grades 7–9
   Five children will not reveal what they know about a German pilot and a German machine gun.

**Wiesel, Elie (Trans. by Frances Frenaye)**
*Dawn*
[Palestine]
Bantam 1982 [1961]
Grades 9–12
   A young survivor of the Nazis is ordered to execute a British hostage as a reprisal for the murder of a Palestinian prisoner and must face the morality of the situation.

**Wiesel, Elie**
*The Gates of the Forest*
[Hungary]
Schocken 1989 [1966]
Grades 10–12
   A Jewish boy escapes from the Nazis and pretends to be a deaf mute.

Ziemian, Joseph (Trans. by Janina David)
*The Cigarette Sellers of Three Crosses Square*
[Poland]
Avon 1977
Grades 6–9
　A group of Jewish children manage to survive the Holocaust through ingenuity, courage, and help from the Poles.

## 1946–1990

Achebe, Chinua
*No Longer at Ease*
[Africa]
Fawcett 1990 [1961]
Grades 10–12
　A young man in Lagos is torn between old and new ways.

Alireza, Marianne
*At the Drop of a Veil*
[Saudi Arabia]
Houghton 1973
Grades 10–12
　An American girl becomes part of a harem.

Allende, Isabel (Trans. by Magda Bogin)
*The House of the Spirits*
[Chile]
Knopf 1985
Grades 10–12
　This is an epic tale of a South American family and three generations of women that keep the household together.

Awret, Irene
*Days of Honey*
[Tunisia]
Schocken 1986
Grades 9–12
　This is a story about growing up in Tunisia.

Baker, Jeannie
*Where the Forest Meets the Sea*
[Australia]
Greenwillow 1988
Grades 6–10
　A boy and his father visit a rain forest and learn about its past. The last page is a frightening look at the future.

Bennett, Jack
*The Voyage of the Lucky Dragon*
[Vietnam]
Prentice 1982
Grades 7–10
　The story chronicles the escape of a family to Indonesia, Singapore, and finally Australia.

Bergman, Tamar (Trans. by Hillel Halkin)
*The Boy from over There*
[Israel]
Houghton 1988
Grades 4–7
　A Polish orphan is taken by his uncle to a kibbutz and helps in the fight during the 1947 war.

Berry, James
*A Thief in the Village and Other Stories of Jamaica*
[Jamaica]
Puffin 1990
Grades 7–12
　Readers come to understand a subsistence society and the ties of family and community.

Bess, Clayton
*Story for a Black Night*
[Liberia]
Houghton 1982
Grades 5–8
　A father tells his children about his childhood and in the process clearly depicts family and community life.

**Bruckner, Karl (Trans. by Frances Lobb)**
*The Day of the Bomb*
[Japan]
Van Nostrand 1962
Grades 6–12
    A girl survives the bombing of Hiroshima only to find ten years later that she did not escape its effects.

**Buck, Pearl S.**
*Matthew, Mark, Luke and John*
[Korea]
John Day 1967
Grades 3–5
    This is the story of outcast orphans who were fathered by U.S. soldiers stationed in Korea.

**Caras, Roger Mara**
*Simba*
[Africa]
Holt 1956
Grades 7–12
    In depicting the life of an African lion from birth to death, the author shows the connection of people, land, and animals.

**Carter, Peter**
*Bury the Dead*
[Germany]
Farrar 1987
Grades 7–9
    When her grandmother's brother arrives from West Berlin, the lives of a girl and her family, who live in East Berlin, are changed dramatically and disastrously.

**Chen, Yuan-Tsung**
*The Dragon's Village*
[China]
Penguin 1981
Grades 9–12
    A girl spends her teen years as a revolutionary.

**Clark, Ann Nolan**
*To Stand against the Wind*

[Vietnam]
Viking 1978
Grades 5–8
    In recording his memoirs for his descendants, a boy remembers his valley and hamlet and the wreckage of the Vietnam War.

**Cliff, Michelle**
*No Telephone to Heaven*
[Jamaica]
Vintage 1989
Grades 9–12
    The novel deals with colonialism, mythology, race, and politics.

**Coetzee, J. M.**
*Life and Times of Michael K*
[South Africa]
Penguin 1985
Grades 10–12
    This novel presents a clear picture of the problems facing South Africans.

**Cohen, Miriam**
*Born to Dance Samba*
[Brazil]
Harper 1984
Grades 4–7
    A girl gets ready for the annual carnival in Rio and being chosen queen of the samba.

**Cortazar, Julio (Trans. by Gregory Rabasson)**
*Hopscotch*
[France and Argentina]
Pantheon 1987
Grades 10–12
    A man has many adventures in Paris and Argentina.

**Costantini, Humberto (Trans. by Norman Thomas di Giovanni)**
*The Long Night of Francisco Sanctis*
[Argentina]
Harper 1985
Grades 10–12

An average middle-class man is caught between his conscience and his need for security.

**Degens, T.**
*Transport 7-41-R*
[Germany]
Dell 1974
Grades 6–9

A refugee girl travels through post-World War II Germany and the trip is both shocking and frightening.

**Degens, T.**
*The Visit*
[Germany]
Viking 1982
Grades 6–9

At a family reunion a girl reads the diary of her aunt who was a member of the Hitler Youth and clearly sees the differences between Nazi Germany and Germany today.

**Desai, Anita**
*Clear Light of Day*
[India]
Penguin 1986
Grades 10–12

Sisters are reunited in Old Delhi.

**de Trevino, Elizabeth**
*Borton Turi's Poppa*
[Poland and Italy]
Farrar 1968
Grades 6–8

After World War II, because of the promise of a job, a violin maker and his son walk from Hungary to Italy without identification papers.

**Dillon, Elis**
*The Island of Ghosts*
[Ireland]
Scribner 1989
Grades 7–9

On the island of Inishglass off the Galway coast, modern-day inhabitants live much like

their ancestors in this exciting tale about two boys and their tutor who intends to "kidnap" them.

**Dunn, Mary Lois**
*The Man in the Box*
[Vietnam]
McGraw 1968
Grades 6–9

A young Montagnard boy rescues an American prisoner from the Vietcong and tries to get him back to his military camp.

**Emecheta, Buchi**
*The Bride Price*
[Nigeria]
Braziller 1983 [1976]
Grades 6–10

An Ibo girl and her teacher fall in love, not-withstanding a tribal rule against such practices.

**Fenton, Edward**
*The Morning of the Gods*
[Greece]
Delacorte 1987
Grades 7–12

In 1974 a girl visits the village from which her mother came and learns what it is like to live in a military dictatorship.

**Forman, James**
*Ring the Judas Bell*
[Greece]
Farrar 1965
Grades 9–12

During the Greek Civil War the Andarte continue to fight and family loyalties are torn apart.

**Gaan, Margaret**
*Blue Mountain*
[China]
Dodd 1987
Grades 9–12

The story focuses on adventures in Shanghai's underworld.

**Gaan, Margaret**
*Little Sister*
[China]
Dodd 1983
Grades 7–10

A third generation Chinese-American girl visits Singapore at the beginning of a political rebellion and learns about her family.

**George, Jean Craighead**
*Shark beneath the Reef*
[Mexico]
Harper 1989
Grades 7–9

A 14-year-old boy living in Baja California dreams of catching a shark. He must also decide if he wants to be a fisherman like the rest of his family or study marine biology.

**Gilmore, Kate**
*Remembrance of the Sun*
[Iran]
Houghton 1986
Grades 7–12

An American girl falls in love with an Iranian boy in the last year of the Shah's regime.

**Ginzburg, Eugenia (Trans. by Ian Boland)**
*Within the Whirlwind*
[USSR (Russia)]
Harcourt 1981
Grades 10–12

Love and survival is possible in a Soviet labor camp.

**Godden, Rumer**
*The Peacock Spring*
[India]
Penguin 1986 [1975]
Grades 9–12

An American girl goes to New Delhi to join her diplomat father and has to adjust to a completely different way of life.

**Gordon, Sheila**
*Waiting for the Rain*
[South Africa]
Orchard 1987
Grades 7–9

Two boys, one black and one white, grow up as close friends but politics change their relationship.

**Graham, Gail**
*Crossfire: A Vietnam Novel*
[Vietnam]
Pantheon 1972
Grades 7–10

An American soldier finds four children who are trying to go to Saigon after all villagers have been massacred. In the end all five die.

**Greene, Graham**
*The Quiet American*
[Vietnam]
Penguin 1977 [1955]
Grades 10–12

During the last days of the French occupation an arrogant, firm, principled American causes trouble.

**Haugaard, Erik C.**
*The Little Fishes*
[Italy]
Houghton 1967
Grades 6–8

The effects of World War II are felt by the children in an Italian town.

**Ho, Mingfong**
*Rice Without Rain*
[Thailand]
Lothrop 1990
Grades 7–9

A 17-year-old girl listens to university students who want to modernize her rural village. She does not realize that to further their cause they are willing to destroy her way of life.

**Huynh, Quang Nhuong**
*The Land I Lost*
[Vietnam]
Harper 1982
Grades 6–9

This book contains a series of stories based on the author's adventures in rural Vietnam.

**Jenkins, Lyll Becerra de**
*The Honorable Prison*
[South America]
Dutton 1988
Grades 9–12

When their journalist father is put under house arrest, this Latin-American family must lead a segregated life.

**Jenness, Ayllette and Lisa W. Kroeber**
*A Life of Their Own*
[Guatemala]
Crowell 1975
Grades 5–8

This is the story of the social life and customs of a Central-American Indian family.

**Jones, Toeckey**
*Go Well, Stay Well*
[South Africa]
Harper 1980
Grades 7–9

Two 15-year-old girls, one black and one white, become friends in spite of the apartheid system.

**Jones, Toeckey**
*Skindeep*
[South Africa]
Harper 1986
Grades 7–9

An 18-year-old well-to-do girl falls in love with a fellow student not knowing that he is a coloured passing for white.

**Kattan, Naim (Trans. by Sheila Fischman)**
*Farewell, Babylon*

[Iraq]
Taplinger 1980
Grades 10–12

A Jew is exiled from Iraq.

**Kay, Mara**
*The Burning Candle*
[Yugoslavia]
Lothrop 1968
Grades 6–9

A girl is torn between her religious convictions and the oppression of the Communist party.

**Kemal, Yashar (Trans. by Edouard Roditi)**
*Memed, My Hawk*
[Turkey]
Pantheon 1982
Grades 10–12

A modern-day Robin Hood helps the peasants.

**Kim, Yong-ik**
*Blue in the Seed*
[Korea]
Little 1964
Grades 4–6

A boy, unlike the other children in his village, has blue eyes.

**Kim, Yong-ik**
*The Shoes from Yang San Valley*
[Korea]
Doubleday 1970
Grades 4–6

A pair of brocade shoes helps an 11-year-old orphan remember the parents he lost in the war.

**Lapierre, Dominique (Trans. by Kathryn Spink)**
*The City of Joy*
[India]
Doubleday 1985
Grades 10–12

The novel takes place in a Calcutta slum and the reader experiences the despair and suffering that permeates the story.

**Laye, Camara**
*The Dark Child*
[Africa]
Farrar 1954
Grades 10–12

    A boy grows up in a Guinea village.

**Levitin, Sonia**
*The Return*
[Ethiopia/Sudan/Israel]
Atheneum 1987
Grades 5–10

    A 15-year-old Ethiopian Jewish girl and her brother and sister travel from their mountain home to Sudan and are then airlifted to Israel.

**Lord, Bette B.**
*Spring Moon*
[China]
Avon 1982
Grades 7–10

    Through the eyes of a girl the reader sees five generations of change.

**Major, Kevin**
*Hold Fast*
[Canada]
Delacorte 1980
Grades 7–9

    When their parents are killed, two brothers are separated. One goes to the city to live with relatives and the other goes to their grandfather in a Newfoundland village.

**Mangurian, David**
*Children of the Incas*
[Peru]
Four Winds 1979
Grades 3–6

    A poor Quechua Indian boy grows up in a Peruvian village near Lake Titicaca and describes his life.

**Markandaya, Kamala**
*Nectar in a Sieve*

[India]
New American Library 1954
Grades 9–12

    A girl marries a peasant farmer in southern India and is beset by the problems of industrialization.

**Mathabane, Mark**
*Kaffir Boy*
[South Africa]
Signet 1989
Grades 9–12

    Told in first person, this is the story of a boy growing up under apartheid with poverty, humiliation, and hope.

**Matsubara, Hisako**
*Cranes at Dusk*
[Japan]
Doubleday 1985
Grades 9–12

    After World War II a 10-year-old girl is torn between her parents who try to readjust their lives. The mother tries to hold on to long-held traditions while the father tries to change some of his ideas.

**Mehta, Ved**
*Sound-shadows of the New World*
[India and United States]
Norton 1986
Grades 10–12

    A 15-year-old blind boy leaves India to attend school in Arkansas and experiences a clash of cultures.

**Mishima, Yukio (Trans. by Meredith Weatherby)**
*The Sound of Waves*
[Japan]
Putnam 1981 [1956]
Grades 10–12

    This is a tender love story set in a small village.

**Mo, Timothy**
*Sour Sweet*

[United Kingdom (England)]
Vintage 1985
Grades 10–12

A Chinese immigrant family in London has to contend with government bureaucracy and a secret society.

**Moeri, Louise**
*The Forty-Third War*
[Central America]
Houghton 1989
Grades 6–8

During three days of civil strife a 12-year-old boy and his two friends are kidnapped by revolutionaries and one of them ends up a confirmed revolutionary.

**Naidoo, Beverly**
*Chain of Fire*
[South Africa]
Lippincott 1990
Grades 5–8

The people in a village are to be moved to "the homeland" against their will and the villagers choose to resist.

**Naidoo, Beverly**
*Journey to Jo'burg*
[South Africa]
Lippincott 1986
Grades 4–7

A brother and sister walk to Johannesburg to find their mother who is working there and, in the process, come to understand apartheid clearly.

**Naipaul, V. S.**
*A Bend in the River*
[Africa]
Vintage 1989
Grades 10–12

An uprooted Indian lives in an isolated town at the bend of an African river.

**Narayan, R. K. Malgudi**
*Days*
[India]
Penguin 1985
Grades 10–12

This is a portrayal of life in a small southern town in India.

**Ofek, Uriel**
*Smoke over Golan*
[Israel]
Harper 1979
Grades 4–7

This is a novel about the 1973 Yom Kippur War. A boy whose parents are away is forced to protect his family's farm. The issues are clearly drawn and the reader is part of the conflict that has no right and wrong sides.

**Osborne, Leone Neal**
*Than Hoa of Vietnam*
[Vietnam]
McGraw 1966
Grades 4–6

A boy wants to go to school but must take care of his sister while his parents work in the rice fields.

**Oz, Amos (Trans. by author and Penelope Farmer)**
*Soumchi*
[Israel]
Harper 1981
Grades 5–8

An 11-year-old boy living in Jerusalem tells the story of what happened to him in World War II.

**Paton, Alan**
*Cry the Beloved Country*
[South Africa]
Scribner 1982 [1948]
Grades 9–12

A Zulu parson comes to racially divided Johannesburg to search for his son who is accused of murder.

**Prochazkova, Iva (Trans. by E. D. Crawford)**
*The Season of Secret Wishes*
[Czechoslovakia]
Lothrop 1989
Grades 5–8
 A girl comes to understand the suppression of the government but does not let it ruin her disposition.

**Rau, Margaret**
*Holding up the Sky*
[China]
Lodestar 1983
Grades 5–8
 This is a story about young people who live in different parts of China today.

**Ridgeway, John**
*Road to Osambre*
[Peru]
Penguin 1987
Grades 9–12
 A child's life is saved.

**Rivabella, Omar (Trans. by Paul and Omar Rivabella)**
*Requiem for a Woman's Soul*
[Argentina]
Random 1986
Grades 10–12
 A priest pieces together the shreds of a young woman's diary that chronicles her abduction and torture by the authorities.

**Robinson, Margaret**
*A Woman of Her Tribe*
[Canada]
Scribner 1990
Grades 7–12
 When her mother's job takes a half-English half-Nootka girl to school in British Columbia and away from her village, she has questions about who she is and where she belongs.

**Rochman, Hazel (ed.)**
*Somehow Tenderness Survives*
[South Africa]
Harper 1988
Grades 8–12
 These are ten short stories by black and white South African authors about apartheid.

**Rosen, Billi**
*Andi's War*
[Greece]
Dutton 1989
Grades 5–8
 Neighbors and families are pitted against each other in the Greek Civil War.

**Rush, Norman**
*Whites*
[Botswana]
Knopf 1986
Grades 9–12
 This is a collection of stories about whites and blacks who are caught in a clash of cultures.

**Sacks, Margaret**
*Beyond Safe Boundaries*
[South Africa]
Lodestar 1989
Grades 7–9
 During the 1950s and 1960s a girl comes to see the unfairness of apartheid.

**Say, Allen**
*The Inn-Keeper's Apprentice*
[Japan]
Harper 1979
Grades 6–8
 A boy is getting ready to emigrate to the United States after World War II.

**Schami, Rafik (Trans. by Rika Lesser)**
*A Handful of Stars*
[Syria]
Dutton 1990
Grades 7–10

Using a journal format, a boy's daily life is recorded from ages four through eighteen as he publishes an underground newspaper, goes to jail, and falls in love.

**Skarmeta, Antonio (Trans. by Katherine Silver)**
*Burning Patience*
[Chile]
Pantheon 1987
Grades 10–12
A funny and sad story of adolescent love is set against the recent political intrigues.

**Smith, Mary Anne**
*Tirone*
[Cameroon]
Morrow 1987
Grades 6–8
Two girls serving in the Peace Corps in Cameroon find their friendship devastated because one of them becomes involved with victims of the Mideast War.

**Smith, Rukshana**
*Sumitra's Story*
[United Kingdom (England)]
Coward 1983
Grades 9–12
East Indian immigrants have a lot of adjusting to do and a young girl is torn between her affectionate but controlling family and freedom and bigotry in her new homeland.

**Smith, Wilbur**
*A Time to Die*
[Zimbabwe and Mozambique]
Random 1990
Grades 9–12
A big game hunting expedition is caught between two tribal armies.

**Solzhenitsyn, Aleksandr**
*One Day in the Life of Ivan Denisovich*
[USSR (Russia)]
Bantam 1981 [1963]

Grades 9–12
The novel depicts one day of survival in a Siberian prison camp.

**Southall, Ivan**
*Josh*
[Australia]
Macmillan 1988
Grades 7–9
A 14-year-old boy who lives in the city comes to understand the life led by his ancestors.

**Staples, Suzanne Fisher**
*Shabanu: Daughter of the Wind*
[Pakistan]
Knopf 1989
Grades 7–12
A 12-year-old girl, the younger daughter in a family of camel herders who live in the Cholistan Desert, must face an arranged marriage to a wealthy older man with three wives.

**Szabo, Tamas (Trans. by David Hughes)**
*Boy on the Rooftop*
[Hungary]
Peter Smith 1958
Grades 9–12
An Hungarian boy lives through the 1956 revolution.

**Szymusiak, Molyda (Trans. by Linda Cloverdale)**
*The Stones Cry Out*
[Cambodia]
Hill 1986
Grades 10–12
A girl manages to survive the war.

**Thiele, Colin**
*Fight against Albatross Two*
[Australia]
Harper 1976
Grades 7–9
When an offshore oil well explodes, life in a fishing village is completely changed.

**Thornton, Lawrence**
*Imagining Argentina*
[Argentina]
Doubleday 1987
Grades 10–12
 A Buenos Aires playwright finds that he can "see" what happened to those who disappeared during the recent military regime.

**Townsend, Peter**
*A Girl in the White Ship*
[Vietnam]
Holt 1983
Grades 9–12
 A 13-year-old flees the country.

**Trease, Geoffrey**
*A Flight of Angels*
[United Kingdom (England)]
Lerner 1989
Grades 4–6
 Four youngsters from Nottingham are studying the sixteenth-century sandstone caves under the city when they discover a walled-up alcove in the cellar of a shop owned by the parents of one of the children.

**Unger, Douglas**
*El Yanqui*
[Argentina]
Harper 1986
Grades 9–12
 A drug-using American teenager is adopted by a wealthy family through a student-exchange program and must learn to deal with different customs and values.

**Uris, Leon**
*Exodus*
[Israel]
Bantam 1983 [1958]
Grades 9–12
 The novel centers on the founding of Israel.

**Wartski, Maureen**
*A Boat to Nowhere*
[Vietnam]
Westminster 1980
Grades 5–8
 The Vietcong take over a peaceful community to reeducate the people to communism. A boy helps an old man and his grandchildren escape on a fishing boat.

**Watkins, Yoko Kawashima**
*So Far from the Bamboo Grove*
[Korea and Japan]
Puffin 1990
Grades 5–9
 The lives of a girl and her family are destroyed during the civil war and they escape to Japan.

**Watson, James**
*Talking in Whispers*
[Chile]
Knopf 1984
Grades 7–12
 A 16-year-old runs away from a junta.

**Watson, Lyall**
*Lightning Bird*
[Africa]
Touchstone 1983
Grades 6–8
 A boy travels alone in the bush.

**Wojciechowska, Maia**
*Shadow of A Bull*
[Spain]
Atheneum 1964
Grades 5–8
 A boy is forced to become a bullfighter.

**Note:** For good readers who enjoy reading we recommend the following books by James A. Michener. They have separate annotations because most of these works span large portions of the history of a place and therefore do not fit conveniently into any specified time period.

**Michener, James A.**
*The Covenant*
[South Africa]
Fawcett 1988 [1980]
Grades 10–12

This is the story of the development of South Africa that was carved out of the African wilderness.

_____.
*Poland*
[Poland]
Fawcett 1984
Grades 10–12

The story of militant Polish farmers and their grievances and demands. Covers the time period between 1241 through 1981.

_____.
*The Source*
[Israel]
Fawcett 1988 [1965]
Grades 10–12

Through the discoveries of an archaeological expedition the reader comes to see the past and present in Israel.

# APPENDIX

## Publishers' Names and Addresses

**Abelard-Schuman**
666 Fifth Avenue
New York, NY 10019

**Ace Books**
Berkley Publishing Group
200 Madison Avenue
New York, NY 10016

**Aladdin**
Macmillan Publishing Co.
866 Third Avenue
New York, NY 10022

**Alaska Northwest Books**
P.O. Box 3007
Bothell, WA 98041-3007

**Algonquin Books**
Workman Publishing Co.
Box 2225
Chapel Hill, NC 27515

**Amsco School Publications, Inc.**
315 Hudson Street
New York, NY 10013

**Anchor Press**
Doubleday and Co.
666 Fifth Avenue
New York, NY 10103

**Arion Press**
460 Bryant Street
San Francisco, CA 94107

**Atheneum Children's Books**
Macmillan Publishing Co.
866 Third Avenue
New York, NY 10022

**Avon Books**
105 Madison Avenue
New York, NY 10016

**Ballantine Books**
Random House
201 East 50th Street
New York, NY 10022

**Bantam Books**
Books for Young Readers
666 Fifth Avenue
New York, NY 10103

**Barron's Educational Series Inc.**
250 Wireless Boulevard
Hauppauge, NY 11787

**Berkley Publishing**
200 Madison Avenue
New York, NY 10016

**Bradbury Press**
866 Third Avenue
New York, NY 10022

**Braziller, George, Inc.**
60 Madison Avenue
Suite 1001
New York, NY 10010

**Clarion Books**
Houghton Mifflin Co.
52 Vanderbilt Avenue
New York, NY 10017

**Collins-World, Inc.**
Edgewater Books
P.O. Box 40238
Cleveland, OH 44140

**Coward-McCann**
Putnam Publishing Group
200 Madison Avenue
New York, NY 10016

**Creative Arts Book Co.**
833 Bancroft Way
Berkeley, CA 94710

**Criterion Press**
P.O. Box 1014
Torrance, CA 90505

**Crowell**
Harper and Row Junior Books
10 East 53d Street
New York, NY 10022

**Crown Publishers, Inc.**
225 Park Avenue South
New York, NY 10003

**Delacorte Press**
666 Fifth Avenue
New York, NY 10103

**Dell Publishing Co.**
666 Fifth Avenue -
New York NY 10103

**Dial Books for Young Readers**
Two Park Avenue
New York, NY 10016

**Dodd, Mead and Co.**
71 Fifth Avenue
New York, NY 10003

**Doubleday Publishing**
666 Fifth Avenue
New York, NY 10103

**Dutton Children's Books**
E.P. Dutton
2 Park Avenue

New York, NY 10016

**Elsevier Nelson**
Lodestar Books
375 Hudson Street
New York, NY 10014

**Faber and Faber**
50 Cross Street
Winchester, MA 01890

**Farrar, Straus, and Giroux**
19 Union Square West
New York, NY 10003

**Fawcett Publications**
Random House
201 East 50th Street
New York, NY 10022

**Fireside Books**
Simon and Schuster, Inc.
1230 Avenue of the Americas
New York, NY 10021

**Follett Press**
1000 West Washington Boulevard
Chicago, IL 60607

**Four Winds Press**
Macmillan Publishing Co.
866 Third Avenue
New York, NY 10022

**Funk and Wagnalls**
Harper and Row Publishers
10 East 53d Street
New York, NY 10022

**Godine**
David R. Godine Publisher
Horticultural Hall
300 Massachusetts Avenue
Boston, MA 02115

**Greenwillow Books**
William Morrow and Co.
105 Madison Avenue
New York, NY 10016

**Hall**
G. K. Hall and Co.
Macmillan Publishing Co.
70 Lincoln Street
Boston, MA 02111

**Harcourt Brace Jovanovich**
1250 Sixth Avenue
San Diego, CA 92101

**Harbinger House**
3131 North Country Club
Suite 106
Tucson, AZ 85716

**Harper and Row**
10 East 53d Street
New York, NY 10022

**Harvey House**
20 Waterside Plaza
New York, NY 10010

**Hawthorn Press**
Anthroposophic Press Inc.
Box 94-A-1
RR 4
Hudson, NY 12534

**Heinemann Books**
Reed Publishing Co.
Hanover Street
Portsmouth, NH 03801-3959

**Hendrick-Long Publishing Co.**
4811 West Lovers Lane
Dallas, TX 75209

**Herald Press**
616 Walnut Avenue

Scottdale, PA 15683

**Heritage Books**
1540 E. Pointer Ridge Place
Bowie, MD 20716

**Hill and Wang, Inc.**
19 Union Square West
New York, NY 10003

**Holiday House, Inc.**
18 East 53d Street
New York, NY 10022

**Holt**
Henry Holt and Co.
115 West 18th Street
New York, NY 10011

**Horizon Books**
P.O. Box 3083
Freemont, CA 94539

**Houghton Mifflin Co.**
2 Park Street
Boston, MA 02108

**Jewish Publication Society**
60 East 42d Street
Room 1339
New York, NY 10165

**John Day**
Harper-Collins Publishers
10 East 53d Street
New York, NY 10022

**Knopf**
Alfred A. Knopf, Inc.
Books for Young Readers
201 East 50th Street
New York, NY 10022

**Lerner Publishing Co.**
241 First Avenue, N.

Minneapolis, MN 55401

**Lippincott**
J.B. Lippincott Jr. Books
10 East 53d Street
New York, NY 10022

**Little, Brown, and Co., Inc.**
34 Beacon Street
Boston, MA 02108

**Lodestar Books**
E.P. Dutton and Co.
2 Park Avenue
New York, NY 10016

**Longman, Inc.**
Addison-Wesley Pub. Co.
95 Church Street
White Plains, NY 10601

**Lothrop, Lee, and Shepard**
William Morrow and Co., Inc.
105 Madison Avenue
New York, NY 10016

**Macmillan Publishing Co.**
866 Third Avenue
New York, NY 10022
    and
1200 NW 63d Street
Box 25308
Oklahoma City, OK 73125

**McElderry**
Margaret K. McElderry Books.
Macmillan Publishing Co.
866 Third Avenue, 24th Floor
New York, NY 10022

**McKay, David, Co.**
Random House Inc.
201 East 50th Street
M D 4-6
New York, NY 10022

**Meredith Publishers**
121 Regent Street
Lido Beach, NY 11561

**Modern Library**
Random House Inc.
201 East 50th Street
New York, NY 10022

**Morrow**
William Morrow and Co., Inc.
105 Madison Avenue
New York, NY 10016

**Nelson, Thomas, Publishers**
P.O. Box 141000
Nelson Place at Elm Hill Pike
Nashville, TN 37214

**New American Library**
1633 Broadway
New York, NY 10019

**New Market Press**
18 East 42d Street
New York, NY 10017

**New Mexico Press**
1100 St. Francis Drive
Montoya Bldg.
Santa Fe, NM 87503

**Newton Publishers**
Box 181
Middlebury VT 05753

**Norton, W.W. and Co., Inc.**
500 Fifth Avenue
New York, NY 10110

**Odyssey Press**
Bobbs-Merrill Co.
866 Third Avenue
New York, NY 10002

**Orchard Books**
Franklin Watts Inc.
387 Park Avenue South
New York, NY 10016

**Oxford University Press**
200 Madison Avenue
New York, NY 10016

**Pantheon Books**
Division of Random House Inc.
201 East 50th Street
New York, NY 10022

**Parnassus Imprints**
Box 335
Orleans, MA 02653

**Penguin Books**
Viking Penguin
Children's Books
40 West 23d Street
New York, NY 10010

**Peter Smith Publishers**
6 Lexington Avenue
Magnolia, MA 01930

**Philomel Books**
The Putnam and Grosset Group
200 Madison Avenue
New York, NY 10010

**Plume**
New American Library
Subsidiary of Pearson,Inc.
1633 Broadway
New York, NY 10019

**Prentice-Hall**
Simon and Schuster Books
1230 Avenue of the Americas
New York, NY 10020

**Puffin Books**
40 West 23d Street
New York, NY 10010

**Putnam and Grosset Group**
200 Madison Avenue
New York, NY 10016

**Queens House**
P.O. Box 145
Dana Point, CA 92629

**Random House Books**
201 East 50th Street
New York, NY 10022

**Schocken Books**
Random House, Inc.
201 East 50th Street
New York, NY 10022

**Scholastic Books**
730 Broadway
New York, NY 10003

**Scribner**
Charles Scribner's Sons
Macmillan Children's Books
866 Third Avenue
New York, NY 10022

**Seabury Press, Inc.**
Harper Religious Books
151 Union Street
San Francisco, CA 94111

**Seaver Books**
Arcade Publishing Inc.
141 Fifth Avenue
New York, NY 10010

**Signet Books**
New American Library
Subsidiary of Pearson, Inc.
1633 Broadway

New York, NY 10019

**Silver Burdett Press**
Simon and Schuster Inc.
Prentice-Hall Bldg.
Englewood Cliffs, NJ 07632

**Simon and Schuster Books**
1230 Avenue of the Americas
New York, NY 10020

**St. Martin's Press**
Macmillan Publishing Co.
175 Fifth Avenue
New York, NY 10010

**Summit Press**
18 Black Hawk Trail
Savannah, GA 31411

**Sunburst Books**
Farrar, Straus, and Giroux
19 Union Square West
New York, NY 10003

**Taplinger Publishing Co.**
Box 1324
New York, NY 10185

**Ticknor and Fields**
Houghton Mifflin Co.
215 Park Avenue South
New York, NY 10003

**Touchstone Books**
Simon and Schuster Inc.
1230 Avenue of the Americas
New York, NY 10021

**Ungar, F Book—Continuum**
Harper and Row Publishers
10 East 53d Street
New York, NY 10022

**University of Kentucky Press**
Lexington, KY 10506 0039

**University of Washington Press**
P.O. Box 50096
Seattle, WA 98145-5096

**Vanguard Books**
1011 Fourth Street
Suite 305
Santa Monica, CA 90403

**Van Nostrand, D.**
Shepard, Joyce
13 Sixpence Way
Coronado, CA 92118

**Victor Gollancz**
Gollancz Ltd.
Houghton Mifflin Inc.
1 Beacon Street
Boston, MA 02108

**Viking Kestrel**
Viking Penguin Children's Books
40 West 23d Street
New York, NY 10010

**Vintage Books**
201 East 50th Street
New York, NY 10022

**Walck, Henry Z., Inc.**
David Mckay Co., Inc.
201 East 50th Street
New York, NY 10022-7703

**Walker and Company**
720 Fifth Avenue
New York, NY 10019

**Warne**
Frederick Warne
40 West 23d Street
New York, NY 10010

**Warner Jewish Books**
Little, Brown and Co., Inc.
34 Beacon Street
Boston, MA 02108

**Watts**
Franklin Watts
387 Park Avenue South
New York, NY 10016

**Wesleyan Enterprises, Inc.**
101 North Colorado Street
P.O. Box 908
Chandler AZ 85244

**Westminster/John Knox Press**
100 Witherspoon Street
Louisville, KY. 40202-1396

**Whitman**
Albert Whitman and Co.
5747 West Howard Street
Niles, IL 60648

**World**
William Collins and World Pub. Co.
2080 West 117 Street
Cleveland, OH 44111

# Notes

# Notes

# Notes

# Notes